MW00763944

Images for a Generation Doomed

Images for a Generation Doomed

The Films and Career of Gregg Araki

KYLO-PATRICK R. HART

LEXINGTON BOOKS
A division of
ROWMAN & LITTLEFIELD PUBLISHERS, INC.
Lanham • Boulder • New York • Toronto • Plymouth, UK

Published by Lexington Books
A division of Rowman & Littlefield Publishers, Inc.
A wholly owned subsidary of The Rowman & Littlefield Publishing Group, Inc.
4501 Forbes Boulevard, Suite 200, Lanham, Maryland 20706
http://www.lexingtonbooks.com

Estover Road, Plymouth PL6 7PY, United Kingdom

British Library Cataloguing in Publication Information Available

Library of Congress Cataloging-in-Publication Data

Images for a generation doomed : the films and career of Gregg Araki / Kylo-Patrick R.
Hart.
     p. cm.
   Includes filmography.
   Includes bibliographical references and index.
   ISBN 978-0-7391-3997-4 (cloth : alk. paper)
   ISBN 978-0-7391-3999-8 (electronic)
   1. Araki, Gregg—Criticism and interpretation. I. Hart, Kylo-Patrick R. II. Title.
   PN1998.3.A65H37 2009
   791.4302'33092—dc22   2009033981

Printed in the United States of America

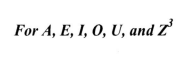

For A, E, I, O, U, and Z^3

Contents

Preface

The first time I viewed *The Doom Generation*, Gregg Araki's 1995 film, I absolutely hated it. I stumbled upon it during my early years of doctoral study at the University of Michigan, while supporting myself by managing a video store on the weekends, and because I found its cover-box text and images to be so intriguing, I ended up taking it home. As I watched it, I found its narrative to be a bit too fractured and surreal, its dialogue to be a bit too evidently scripted and pretentious, its characters to be a bit too lackluster and stereotypical, and its entirely unexpected, extremely brutal concluding bloodbath to be unnecessarily shocking rather than truly compelling. As its closing credits (thankfully!) started to roll, I immediately classified the work in my mind as a leading example of cinematic trash and went on with my everyday life.

In the days following that first viewing experience, however, I could not get Araki's film—its sexually charged narrative developments, its most amusingly noteworthy lines of dialogue, the angst-filled interactions among its central characters, and particularly its blood-soaked ending—out of my mind. As I reflected further on both its manifest and latent contents, I started to appreciate the way that the work's rawness, aggressive energy, and treatment of nihilistic plot developments and themes substantially challenge hegemonic conceptions of ideology and social order as well as repressive sexual and gender roles. I began to realize that Araki's use of film grammar to convey a "gay sensibility" and his reworking of established genre expectations to serve queer storytelling goals rendered the film potentially quite subversive. Less than a week after I had initially encountered the film, it dawned on me clearly that *The Doom Generation* isn't really cinematic trash after all, even though it may look that way on its surface. Instead, it actually communicates a powerful, sobering message about the threats of religious and social conservatism to the well-being of all individuals who can be regarded as "deviant" in any way from the hegemonic mainstream status quo. As a result, I ended up watching the film again (and again, and then again), and it has since become one of my all-time favorite films.

My newfound enthusiasm for the cultural treasure that is *The Doom Generation* motivated me to seek out and view Araki's other films. While writing my book *The AIDS Movie: Representing a Pandemic in Film and Television*, I got to know the contents of Araki's AIDS road movie, *The Living End* (1992), quite intimately, and I found it to offer a unique brand of realism with regard to the cinematic exploration of the lives of contemporary queer individuals and people with HIV/AIDS as well as provocative on-screen images of romantic and sexual relationships that border at times on the pornographic. I appreciated the way that *Totally F***ed Up* (1993), with its focus on the search for happiness and meaning in their everyday lives by a small group of gay and lesbian teens, continued to foreground a variety of human sexualities and sexual practices that have historically been marginalized by mainstream society and rarely encountered in U.S. cinema. I found *Nowhere* (1997), Araki's seemingly hallucinogenic exploration into the realities of life as experienced by contemporary teens of various sexual orientations, to offer a more playful, hormonally charged, and eye-candy-filled viewing experience (even though I found its concluding sequence to be frustrating and entirely unfulfilling). I looked forward with enthusiasm to seeing what the director's future cinematic offerings would be.

During my first year as a new assistant professor, at the start of the new millennium, I decided to teach a course on auteur film directors. Given my appreciation of his unique storytelling approaches and his penchant for exploring (potentially) controversial subject matter and non-heterosexual themes in boundary-pushing ways, I chose, in addition to Ingmar Bergman and other widely revered auteurs, to include Gregg Araki as one of our subjects of study. Because I only had enough time available for the students to view and discuss three Araki films, my plan was for them to analyze *The Living End*, *The Doom Generation*, and *Nowhere*. However, just prior to the week during which we were to analyze *Nowhere*, I learned that Araki's subsequent film, *Splendor* (1999), about two young men and one young woman who enter into a ménage-à-trois living arrangement, had been released on DVD. I immediately ordered a copy, which arrived on the day of our class meeting. As a result, I did not have an opportunity to view its contents in advance of walking into the classroom. I then gave my students a choice: to view and discuss *Nowhere* as originally planned, or to instead view and discuss *Splendor*, with the express disclaimer that I had not yet personally seen it, so I had no idea what sorts of (potentially extreme) Arakian imagery and plot developments it might contain. The students opted for *Splendor* and I sat back, a bit apprehensively, to view it along with them, fearing what instances of explicit dialogue or violent and sexual acts it might contain. To all of our surprise (and, quite frankly, subsequent disappointment), the contents of *Splendor* were far more tame than any of us ever imagined they would be—two attractive guys and a similarly attractive young woman living together, sleeping together in the same bed, and having sex in that bed and nothing at all happens between the two guys? There's not even any romantic or sexual attraction evident between the two men at any point in the film?

When all was said and done, *Splendor* ended up feeling like it was made by a different director entirely, and it left my students and I wondering what we should make of a previously boundary-pushing auteur director and New Queer Cinema pioneer whose most recent cinematic offering was both the "straightest" and most mainstream of his career up to that point. Accordingly, this book pertaining to the films and career trajectory of Gregg Araki is intended, at least in part, to begin to answer that very important question. It is also intended to offer noteworthy insights into Araki's various cinematic offerings, from *Three Bewildered People in the Night* (1987) to *Smiley Face* (2007) and everything in between.

Acknowledgments

I would like to thank Mary Desjardins, J. Martin Favor, and Klaus Milich for their invaluable feedback on my early drafts of this book manuscript.

I wish to acknowledge all of the smile-filled companionship and emotional support provided to me by the members of the entire Hart pack (past and present) during the various stages of this project (and beyond).

I would also like to thank all of the following individuals who have, knowingly or unknowingly, contributed to the success of this project in meaningful ways: Richard Allen, Jack Beckham, Richard Benjamin, Catherine Burke, Cindy Cantrell, Richard Capone, Gregory Caybut, Ross Chambers, Donna Clapp, Lauren Clarke, Catherine DiFonso, Tangela Diggs, Robert Franks, Christine Gagne, Michelle Givertz, Patricia Gonzalez, John Head, Steve Johnson, Victoria Johnson, Dorothy Kato, Joseph Kato, Melissa Kato, Alix Kneifel, Beverly Kuo-Hamilton, Amy Lawrence, Kellie Lee, Barbara Lopez-Mayhew, David Mackey, Daryl McDaniel, Andrea Mullarkey, Wole Ojurongbe, Fawn Ouellette, Christine Pace, Brian Patrick, Donald Pease, Elizabeth Powers, Susan Raber, Timothy Roggeman, Lisa Siegler, Todd Smilovitz, Kaye Weitzman, Marla Weitzman, Brice Wheeler, Metasebia Woldemariam, S. Brandon Wu, and Amit Zohar.

Finally, I wish to thank Gregg Araki for creating, over the past two decades, one of the most intriguing cumulative bodies of work ever to be captured on film.

"Cinematic Trash or Cultural Treasure? Conflicting Viewer Reactions to the Extremely Violent World of Bisexual Men in Gregg Araki's 'Heterosexual Movie' *The Doom Generation*" by Kylo-Patrick R. Hart was originally published in *Journal of Bisexuality* 7.1 (January 1, 2007) and is reprinted by permission of the publisher (Taylor & Francis Ltd., http://www.tandf.co.uk/journals).

Chapter 1
Gregg Araki and the New Queer Cinema

Two attractive, HIV-positive young men, feeling that they are victims of the
sexual revolution, embark on an L.A. shopping spree using a stolen credit
card. Walking down the street carrying a new boom box and armfuls of additional items, they stop and engage in a quick kiss. Accosted by a neo-Nazi
punk who does not appreciate their public display of affection, the pair is informed what AIDS stands for: "Adios, infected dick suckers." One member
of the pair wants to just walk away and avoid escalation of this confrontation; the other member glares at the punk with rage in his eyes. Ultimately,
the two men walk off in one direction and the punk heads in the other. Sec
onds later, however, one of the HIV-positive men chases the punk down the
street, wielding the boom box as a weapon, and beats him repeatedly over
the head with it, leaving the punk for dead.

Elsewhere in Los Angeles, a teenage boy adds condiments to his
Quickie Mart hotdogs as his girlfriend is informed by the Korean male
shopkeeper that she must extinguish her cigarette. She does so by dropping it
to the floor and putting it out with her shoe. Told by the man to pick up the
extinguished remains, the girl responds defiantly, "Eat my fuck." From behind the counter, the shopkeeper pulls a loaded shotgun and aims it at her,
motivating her to comply with his request. She places it into a garbage can
located directly beneath a giant sign that reads, "Shoplifters will be exe-
cuted." Placing his food items on the counter, the boy discovers that his purchase total is $6.66 and that, alas, he does not have his wallet with him. He
looks to his girlfriend for help; she finds that she does not have any money
with her, either. The man repeats the purchase total twice, aiming his gun directly at the couple. Seemingly out of nowhere, a young male drifter the
couple encountered earlier that evening rushes behind the counter, wrestles
with the shopkeeper for control of the gun, and instructs the couple to flee.

1

Suddenly, the shopkeeper's wife enters the struggle occurring behind the counter. The gun is accidentally fired, shooting the shopkeeper's head off of his body—it flies through the air across the store, landing in the tray of hot-dog condiments. Unexpectedly, the eyes on the severed head open and the head itself attempts to speak, a green substance emanating from its mouth. The three young people run off into the night, taking cash from the register, packs of cigarettes, and bottles of beer with them as they depart.

Waiting at an L.A. bus stop, a sexually confused teenage boy smokes a cigarette and overhears the conversation of three loudly dressed valley girls who discuss which guys and girls are sleeping with which guys and girls, either as straight or queer pairings or as part of kinky threeways, as well as one guy who has an especially "dinky weenie." Out of boredom, the boy is about to extinguish his cigarette using the tip of his finger when he glimpses a green-and-yellow space creature directly across the street. Scrambling unsuccessfully with his video camera to capture an image of this alien being, the boy watches in amazement as the creature pulls out a laser gun and vaporizes the three girls, causing them to disappear. Visibly shaken, the teen looks around quickly in all directions. He soon finds that the space creature has also vanished.

The preceding three intriguing scenes can be found in the films *The Living End* (1992), *The Doom Generation* (1995), and *Nowhere* (1997) respectively, all of which were directed by Gregg Araki, the subject of this study. Not only do they provide introductory insights into noteworthy moments from this director's oeuvre, but they simultaneously offer glimpses into the ways that the director's radical/subversive potential and treatment of his subject matter underwent noticeable change over the course of the 1990s, as they became increasingly more playful and tame.

About Gregg Araki and His Films

Over the past two decades, Gregg Araki has emerged as one of the limited number of auteurs working in U.S. cinema today. Having served simultaneously as the writer, director, cinematographer, and editor of his first four feature-length films and relinquished just a bit of that control on the films that followed, he has used the plasticity of the filmic medium to consistently explore the theme of rootless young people who are desperate to connect meaningfully with others and explore their sexualities amid a culture that foregrounds sex, drugs, and (post-punk/industrial) rock 'n' roll in a series of intriguing films aimed substantially at queer audiences. Although it is not always evident from his cinematic creations, Araki is well familiar with the works of noteworthy auteur directors from the first century of cinema, and he has repeatedly identified the French New Wave director Jean-Luc Godard as being one of the most significant influences on his own moviemaking style. About his cinematic works, Araki has said that he would prefer his audience members to be enraged rather than understanding or sympathetic (Levy, *Cinema* 469).

Born on December 17, 1959 in Los Angeles, Araki was raised in Santa Barbara, California and became an enthusiastic participant in the West Coast punk rock scene during the late 1970s and 1980s. He went on to earn a bachelor's degree in film studies at the University of California, Santa Barbara and a master of fine arts degree in film production at the University of Southern California's School of Cinema-Television before making his first two feature-length films, shot and edited on incredibly low budgets (of approximately five thousand dollars each), in the late 1980s.

Araki's first film, shot in black and white, was *Three Bewildered People in the Night* (1987). It explores the emotional love triangle between three young adults: Alicia (played by Darcy Marta), a straight video artist; her live-in boyfriend, Craig (played by John Lacques), an aspiring photographer and actor who remains sexually unsatisfied by her; and David (played by Mark Howell), a performance artist and Alicia's gay best friend. The storyline focuses primarily on the trio's attempts to come to terms with their feelings and their sexualities—including the mutually growing attraction between the two men—amid the backdrop of Greenwich Village apartments, galleries, late-night coffee shops, and empty streets.

His second film, also shot in black and white, was *The Long Weekend (O' Despair)* (1989), which centers on the conversations (primarily about being bored and directionless) and experiences (such as bisexual encounters, infidelity, and potential breakups) of six bewildered young people—three twentysomething college friends (a heterosexual woman, a lesbian, and their gay male friend whom they visit) as well as their past or present lovers—over the course of an extended holiday weekend in Los Angeles. During the three days they spend together, they come to realize that, half a decade after graduation, they remain relatively directionless, confused about life, and unable to successfully recapture the exuberance of their past.

About these two early features, Araki has stated:

> The world as depicted in these films may be a fluorescent shithole of AM/PM minimarts and monolithic parking structures, and relationships themselves may be seen as confounding, confusing, and finally impossible, but the characters in both ultimately love each other and hopefully/hopelessly cling to the possibility of romantic redemption. (Araki, "Filmmaker's" 4)

Neither film received widespread distribution, and they have rarely been
screened to date.

It was Araki's third feature film, *The Living End* (1992), however, that
caught the eye of critics and established him as one of the noteworthy directors of the so-called New Queer Cinema, which emerged in the early
1990s. Made on a twenty-thousand-dollar budget with the working title
"Fuck the World," this offering, which follows the reckless road-trip adventures of two HIV-positive gay men who find liberation in their newfound
health status, features provocative images of bareback gay sex, blowjobs behind the steering wheel, S&M, and related phenomena not frequently seen
up to that point in U.S. cinema, along with seemingly random acts of violence and an almost unwatchable male-on-male rape at gunpoint. Without
question, this is the film that first began to demonstrate the effectiveness of
what I have referred to elsewhere as Araki's post-punk directorial style,
which contributes substantially to the radical/subversive potential of his
various cinematic creations (Hart, "Auteur" 30).

Like punk music in its heyday, *The Living End* and the majority of
Araki's other films to date are readily identifiable by the rawness, aggressive
energy, disconcerting tone, nihilistic themes, and intentional lack of commercial appeal they contain, which result in their embodiment of powerful
impulses pertaining to anarchy and disorder at the same time that the films
ultimately refuse to take themselves or their subject matter too seriously
(Hart, "Auteur" 30-32). Although the punk movement was inherently homophobic despite the reality that it simultaneously and continually produced
and circulated non-normative (or "queer") gender representations (e.g., boys
and young men wearing lipstick and sporting outrageously dyed hairstyles,
girls and young women regularly using vulgar language and demonstrating
related forms of transgressive behavior, etc.), post-punk creative offerings
tend to retain the defining hallmarks of punk offerings while embracing non-
normativity and queerness in its numerous forms (including sexual orientation), rather than perpetuating homophobia. About his groundbreaking work,
Araki himself has indicated:

> *The Living End* is my first effort at directly addressing this subtextually
> submerged side of my cinematic personality. A couple-on-the-run movie in
> the tradition of [Fritz] Lang's *You Only Live Once* [1937], [Nicholas]
> Ray's *They Live by Night* [1949], [Jean-Luc] Godard's *Pierrot le Fou*
> [1965], and [Terrence] Malick's *Badlands* [1974], it is easily my most des-
> perate picture to date. And as much as I loathe the pigeonholing label, it is
> also the most frankly "gay." Reckless and extreme, the film challenges not
> only the conventions established by the genre but those constraints im-
> posed by our virulently homophobic Mainstream Culture as well. . . . For-
> mally/aesthetically/thematically/politically, *The Living End* is without a

doubt the riskiest, most dangerous movie I've attempted. Which is pre-cisely why, of course, I wanted to make it in the first place. (Araki, "Film-maker's" 4)

From there, Araki turned his attention to creating his "teen-apocalypse trilogy," composed of the films *Totally F***ed Up* (1993), *The Doom Generation* (1995), and *Nowhere* (1997). The first of these films follows a half dozen gay and lesbian friends as they search for happiness and meaning in their everyday L.A. existence and are sporadically captured on videotape while doing so as part of a documentary that one of them is making. The second of these films is, like *The Living End*, a road movie; this one explores the encounters of three rootless young people—a dim straight teen, his bored and drug-using girlfriend, and a bisexual drifter—as they push the bounda-ries of sexual experimentation and explore their deepest sexual desires in the aftermath of murdering a Quickie Mart owner and several other individuals. The third and final film in the trilogy provides a day-in-the-life glimpse into the everyday realities of an eighteen-year-old L.A. teen, as he experiences romantic complications with the teenage girl he has been sleeping with (who has a girlfriend named Lucifer on the side), explores bisexual urges with an-other male teen, and has occasional run-ins with a space alien. Over the course of these three films, it becomes apparent that Araki has substantially toned down the extreme sexual images and storylines that garnered him widespread notoriety in the wake of *The Living End*'s release, as both his production budgets and industry expectations for the commercial success of his cinematic offerings continued to grow.

Splendor (1999), Araki's seventh feature film, is a romantic comedy about an aspiring L.A. actress who becomes romantically and sexually in-volved with two very different types of men. Because she cannot choose between them, the three end up living together until she ultimately finds her-self attracted to yet another man. Although viewers might expect some sort of romantic or sexual attraction to become evident between the two men at some point in the narrative (given the contents of Araki's preceding works), no such vibe ever materializes, and the work ends up feeling as if it were made by a different director. Lacking entirely are the director's trademark in-your-face style and extreme sexual/violent images that his fans had come to expect. Just as the New Queer Cinema movement lost is radi-cal/subversive potential over the course of the 1990s, so apparently had Gregg Araki. It remained to be seen whether his filmmaking career had come to an end prior to the start of the new millennium.

About the New Queer Cinema

The term "New Queer Cinema" was coined by B. Ruby Rich to characterize the growing presence of noteworthy queer films, which seized the attention of critics, on the festival circuit in the early 1990s. Such works included *Edward II* (Derek Jarman, 1991), *The Hours and Times* (Christopher Münch, 1991), *My Own Private Idaho* (Gus Van Sant, 1991), *Poison* (Todd Haynes, 1991), *R.S.V.P.* (Laurie Lynd, 1991), *Swoon* (Tom Kalin, 1992), and Gregg Araki's *The Living End* (1992). Although the New Queer Cinema is sometimes also described as the "Queer New Wave," in ways similar to that of the French New Wave of the late 1950s and early 1960s, it is important to note that the new body of queer films demonstrated far less coherence in techniques, aesthetic approaches, narrative strategies, and concerns than that of the preceding French film movement (Beaver 259-61; Rich, "New" 54). What they did share in common, however, was a common style and attitude. With regard to the former, Rich referred to their common style as "'Homo Pomo': there are traces in all of them of appropriation and pastiche, irony, as well as a reworking of history with social constructionism very much in mind. Definitively breaking with older humanist approaches and the films and tapes that accompanied identity politics, these works are irreverent, energetic, alternately minimalistic and excessive" ("New" 54). With regard to the latter, Rich adds that such films are, more than anything else, "full of pleasure" ("New" 54), at least in part because they are filled with defiance.

As Michele Aaron has demonstrated, such defiance in New Queer Cinema films operates on at least five different levels. First, it gives voice to marginalized members of the LGBTQ community as well as to the various subgroups that exist within it through the existence of the films themselves (4). Second, it allows such films to eschew positive imagery, as in offerings such as *The Living End* and *Poison* which (homo)eroticize extreme acts of violence and beautify their criminal characters, allowing them to remain stylishly well-groomed even when they are on the run (4). Third, it motivates such films to restore evidence of non-heterosexuality to representations of historical occurrences, thereby challenging and subverting a homophobic (cinematic) past (4). Fourth, it motivates such films and their makers to defy cinematic convention with regard to content, form, genre, linearity, or even coherence (4-5). Finally, defiance in films of the New Queer Cinema enables them to (symbolically) defy death, at least in terms of how it was defined as a death sentence in the early years of the AIDS pandemic, such as when the HIV-positive characters in *The Living End* derive a powerful liberating effect from the existence of the "ticking time bombs" within them, or when the first individual to die from AIDS in *Zero Patience* (John Greyson, 1994) ends up coming back to life (5).

Aaron concludes this discussion by noting that such defiance, in its various forms, contributes quite substantially to making the corresponding cinematic creations "queer." Accordingly, the meaning of the term "queer," as it has emerged in the field of queer theory over the past two decades, requires articulation here. Taken as a whole, queer theory represents a field of gender studies that, at its core, opposes ready categorization of sexuality and gender in favor of acknowledging that most people's experiences with sexuality and gender are typically ambiguous or fluid (rather than fixed) and remain in flux, at least to some degree, over the course of a lifetime. In doing so, it embraces and celebrates human difference and diversity (with regard to sex/sexuality and otherwise) in their myriad combinations and forms. As a result, the term "queer," once a pejorative word wielded by heterosexuals to denigrate homosexuals, does not apply today solely to individuals who are gay, lesbian, bisexual, or transgendered. Instead, it applies as well to "describe any sexuality not defined as heterosexual procreative monogamy (usually the presumed goal of most classical Hollywood couplings); queers are people (including homosexuals) who do not organize their sexuality according to that rubric" (Benshoff and Griffin 1). In doing so, "queer" challenges patriarchal hegemony's widely shared, culturally influential notion that "only one sexuality (married-straight-white-man-on-top-of-woman-sex-for-procreation-only) is normal and desirable" (Benshoff and Griffin 5–6); offers new ways of thinking about what it means to be "normal," "(in)appropriate," or "deviant"; embraces a wide range of human sexualities and sexual practices that have historically been marginalized by mainstream society (including fetishism, gender bending, masochism, prostitution, and sadism, among numerous others); and offers a way of being in the world that is under continuous revision or permanent becoming. In addition, as Harry Benshoff and Sean Griffin have indicated, the term "queer" can be used to more effectively "define a new generation of people (and the films they make) that resist being labeled into a heterosexual–homosexual binary" (2). Summing up this important and intriguing state of affairs, Michele Aaron has written:

> Queer, a derogatory term leveled at the non-hetero-seeming, was reappropriated in the late 1980s, early 1990s by its victims as a defiant means of empowerment echoing black activists' use of "nigger" in the 1960s. . . . Queer represents the resistance to, primarily, the normative codes of gender and sexual expression—that masculine men sleep with feminine women—but also to the restrictive potential of gay and lesbian sexuality—that only men sleep with men, and women sleep with women. In this way, queer, as a critical concept, encompasses the non-fixity of gender ex-

pression and the non-fixity of both straight and gay sexuality. . . . To be queer now, then, means to be untethered from "conventional" codes of behavior. At its most expansive and utopian, queer contests (hetero- and homo-) normality. . . . In order to understand [New Queer Cinema] fully, one must understand "queer" as critical intervention, cultural product, and political strategy—and [New Queer Cinema] as an art-full manifestation of the overlap between the three. (5-6)

The defiance that is so readily identifiable in works of the New Queer Cinema is widely regarded as being grounded in the realities and context of the AIDS pandemic. As José Arroyo proclaimed in the early 1990s, "AIDS is why there is New Queer Cinema and it is what New Queer Cinema is about" (92). He elaborates:

The fact that HIV may take years to manifest itself and that the pandemic has hit gay communities with devastating force means that, though everyone is a possible seropositive, [queer people's] lived relation to this possibility is much more immanent. This understanding that we are at special risk has affected the construction of our communities, our views of society, sexuality, bodies, relationships, time, history, and culture. . . . [As such], AIDS has affected what amounts to an epistemic shift in gay culture. (91-92)

According to Arroyo, therefore, the emergence of the New Queer Cinema was the direct result of this epistemic shift. Monica Pearl echoes such sentiments when she writes, "New Queer Cinema *is* AIDS cinema: not only because the films . . . emerge out of the time of and the preoccupations with AIDS, but because their narratives and also their formal discontinuities and disruptions are AIDS-related" (23). By this she means that, although the films themselves do not always explicitly address the subject of AIDS, their very form has resulted from the cataclysm of AIDS in Western society, from the various ways that AIDS disrupted both individuals and communities as well as the ways that its resulting realities could be comprehended and expressed, from the disorder and chaos experienced continually by individuals living with and/or dying from the pandemic's widespread existence (24-25). The end result is a new form of "experimental" cinema that substantially reimagines the world as many people had come to know it, one that attempts to accurately reflect the shifts in individual identity that resulted from the existence and ever-lurking threat of AIDS (Schulman 228). The queerness of such films, therefore, stems not only from the subject matter they explore but also from their creative subversion of cinematic convention, narrative storytelling, and film form, as they typically cross boundaries of genre and style and simultaneously feature both excess and minimalism, elements of both Hollywood and avant-garde moviemaking (Wallenberg 140; Benshoff and Griffin 11). In the process, offerings of the New Queer Cinema regularly call into question conceptions of the past and the present with the overarching goal of expressing demand for necessary, long-overdue social change (Wallenberg 139).

Naturally, the New Queer Cinema did not appear out of nowhere. Instead, its appearance was the result of efforts on various fronts, including those by critics in publications such as the *Village Voice*, the *Los Angeles Reader*, and the *Los Angeles Weekly*; grassroots marketing campaigns and word-of-mouth publicity for noteworthy queer films; and the growing popularity of gay and lesbian film festivals over the course of the 1980s (Levy, *Cinema* 460-61). In addition, the frustration, nihilism, and violence evident in so many works of the New Queer Cinema not only resulted from the existence and realities of the AIDS crisis, but they also further influenced the conditions and trajectory of the AIDS crisis as it progressed into its second decade while at the same time possessing noteworthy linkages to artistic creations of the past. Discrimination and stigmatization, typically stemming from fears of the unknown, have been deleterious social forces throughout human history, and they have unquestionably influenced the forms, approaches, and goals of artistic production in all historical eras. By the early 1990s specifically, the visual arts were being used not only as a means of reacting to the AIDS pandemic but also of endeavoring to motivate important social changes with regard to perceptions of non-heterosexual individuals and people with HIV or AIDS in relation to matters of representation, medical science, and individual, political, and social power, utilizing strategies and approaches stemming from those found in preceding artistic creations that have explored subject matter pertaining to otherness and/or epidemic disease. As Mikhaël Elbaz and Ruth Murbach have noted, AIDS "brought back panic, fear, and terror of the Other, condemned and damned, at a time when our Western societies, armed with the miracle of antibiotics, sanitary hygiene, self-surveillance, and the presence of the providential state, seemed to have repressed the fear of death" and resulted in a common cultural repertoire of responses "which has delimited possible reactions to 'diabolical' diseases since the beginning of time: denial, escape, fear, aggression, projection, guilt designation, conspiracy theories, exclusion and stigmatization, and appeals for salvation to moralism and mysticism" (1).

It is perhaps entirely unsurprising, therefore, as Michele Aaron has demonstrated, that films falling into the New Queer Cinema category have been highly contested from their inception, at least in part because they contained unwarranted optimism (with the hope of creating a minor representational revolution that never really materialized), promoted queer villainy (often in the form of the queer psycho-killer) in an era during which homophobic violence was quite prevalent, and suggested that the mass audience had come to embrace and exhibit queer friendliness when that was not necessarily the case (8). In addition, festival planners, theater personnel, and distributors have been criticized for devoting much more enthusiasm and attention to New Queer Cinema films that are by and/or about males rather than those that are by and/or about females (Rich, "New" 54). It is somewhat noteworthy, therefore, that Araki's films tend to oppose this trend to a degree, as he features non-heterosexual female characters in approximately half of the films he has released to date. At the same time, however, these characters are not always represented in positive ways, and they certainly remain overshadowed, and outnumbered, by their surrounding non-heterosexual males. Furthermore, New Queer Cinema offerings have been criticized for being elitist, because they address issues associated so intimately with both queer and postmodern theory (Benshoff and Griffin 12), as well as for ultimately failing to live up to their promise and potential because, over the course of the decade of the 1990s, "a new and *enduring* sector of popular radical work failed to materialize" (Aaron 8). By the end of that decade, the New Queer Cinema had lost its radical impulse and was transformed into a niche market, one that most typically served up ideologically safe and unremarkable films targeted to a very narrow queer audience, including *Bar Girls* (Marita Giovanni, 1994), *Jeffrey* (Christopher Ashley, 1995), *The Incredibly True Adventures of Two Girls in Love* (Maria Maggenti, 1995), *Losing Chase* (Kevin Bacon, 1996), *Hollow Reed* (Angela Pope, 1997), *Kiss Me Guido* (Tony Vitale, 1997), *Billy's Hollywood Screen Kiss* (Tommy O'Haver, 1998), and *High Art* (Lisa Cholodenko, 1998) (Aaron 8). This reality led B. Ruby Rich to question, in the early years of the new millennium, whether the New Queer Cinema has disappeared or is now, in a watered-down version, simply everywhere ("Vision" 43).

About this Book

This book explores the films and career trajectory to date of the noteworthy New Queer Cinema pioneer Gregg Araki. As we have already seen, in the early 1990s this independent director, with his film *The Living End*, emerged as a leading figure in the New Queer Cinema movement. Although he continued to make noteworthy contributions with regard to representing non-heterosexual young people in the age of AIDS in his next two films, *Totally F***ed Up* and *The Doom Generation*, it was already becoming apparent that, as expectations for the commercial success of his offerings continued to grow, the radical/subversive potential of Araki's cinematic creations was beginning to diminish. In fact, Araki's subsequent films, *Nowhere* and *Splendor*, are so toned-down with regard to the director's established in-your-face style and extreme sexual/violent imagery that they no longer appear to contain any sort of radical/subversive potential at all in relation to his early ideological approaches as a New Queer Cinema filmmaker. By the end of the 1990s, Araki's later works had become virtually irrelevant with regard to breaking new ground in cinematic representations of non-heterosexuals. This reality is an important one, because it provides insight into the cultural forces that contributed to the dramatic reduction in the subversive potential of the films produced by a very significant—and formerly quite boundary-pushing—director. In relation to this primary issue, this project will also demonstrate how Araki was, ultimately, successfully able to reestablish his cinematic and cultural relevancy with his 2004 film, *Mysterious Skin*, which garnered him the most favorable critical acclaim of his filmmaking career.

Accordingly, in chapter 2, I explore *The Living End* as an example of influential New Queer Cinema moviemaking with regard to both its representational strengths and shortcomings and the early development of Araki's distinctive filmmaking style. In chapter 3, I examine the first two films of Araki's teen-apocalypse trilogy, *Totally F***ed Up* and *The Doom Generation*, with regard to how they represent both noteworthy continuations of, and deviations from, the emergent post-punk style evident in the director's breakthrough cinematic offering and the radical/subversive potential that is enabled by that style. In chapter 4, I analyze the dramatically reduced radical/subversive potential contained in *Nowhere*, the final offering of the teen-apocalypse trilogy, and *Splendor*, as compared with the director's preceding works and their on-screen representations of non-heterosexuality. In chapter 5, I explore Araki's successful attempts to reestablish his cinematic and cultural relevancy in relation to the approaches and subject matter of contemporary queer cinema with *Mysterious Skin*, a story of self-discovery as two teenage boys deal with the reality of having been sexually abused by their Little League coach years earlier and Araki's first screenplay adaptation, from the acclaimed novel by Scott Heim. Finally, in the afterword, I briefly examine Araki's most recent film, *Smiley Face* (2007), in relation to the contents of his preceding cinematic creations.

In offering advice to emerging filmmakers, Araki has stated, "Don't toe the line and make movies just because you want to be a rock-star director. Make movies that are original, different, personal—that are your unique vision and aren't just copies of the dreck that's already out there" (indieWIRE, par. 11). This book, therefore, proceeds with the assumption that Araki has been following his own advice over the course of his career to date.

Chapter 2
Queerly Making a Splash with
The Living End

The sounds of an aerosol can being shaken and expressed can be heard over a black screen. Seconds later, the spray-painted words "Fuck the World," in bright red letters surrounded by additional graffiti, accost the viewer, accompanied by the abrasive sounds and lyrics of an industrial-tinged song that is (presumably) playing on the nearby Walkman. Still shaking the can, an attractive young man, wearing dark sunglasses and pursing an unlit cigarette in his lips, nods his head in approval and smirks, admiring his textual creation. He then gulps down some whiskey from a bottle of Jack Daniel's and begins dancing in circles euphorically, moving across the landscape overlooking the city of Los Angeles and pausing, in his torn jeans and t-shirt with a leather jacket slung over his shoulder, to throw the can powerfully in the direction of the downtown skyline.

Across town, another attractive, sunglasses-wearing young man starts an old blue car, bearing a "Choose Death" bumper sticker, and proceeds down a palm-tree-lined street. As he drives, the viewer hears the words of his spoken "journal entry for April 14th," which highlights his activities on this day: eating snack cakes for breakfast, buying a new compact disc, and learning the results of his first AIDS test. In flashback, the viewer sees this young man (named Jon, played by Craig Gilmore) vomiting into a public toilet after receiving the news, delivered in an extremely casual manner by a seemingly uncaring doctor, that he is HIV-positive. As he continues to drive, having no idea as to what he will now do, he passes the aforementioned spray-painter (named Luke, played by Mike Dytri), who is now shirtless and also HIV-positive, hitchhiking on the side of the road but does not stop to pick him up. Luke turns to flip Jon off as he drives by.

13

Thus begins *The Living End*, Gregg Araki's 1992 film about two young men who end up hitting the road together, at a time when their seropositivity was widely regarded as an automatic death sentence, after Luke, the street hustler with a hair-trigger temper, (likely) ends up killing a cop. Jon, the freelance film critic, leaves behind his closest female friend, Darcy (played by Darcy Marta), to worry endlessly about him and his health status in order to travel to San Francisco, and then well beyond, with the sexy drifter he just recently met and slept with. With this film, Araki not only presents a powerful piece of social commentary pertaining to the treatment of non-heterosexuals and people with AIDS at its particular historical moment, but he also dramatically further develops his authorial filmmaking style by re-working established film (sub)genres into queer scenarios and providing an endless stream of confrontational, at-times-controversial images and representations of queer characters in its various scenes.

Prior to meeting Jon, for example, Luke is threatened by two serial-killing lesbians who, after picking up the hitchhiker, intend to shoot him and leave him for dead just for kicks. Hours later, following a successful escape, Luke witnesses the fatal stabbing of a bisexual john, with whom he has just engaged in sadomasochistic acts and presumably had sex, after the john's wife returns home, discovers the two guys in bed together, remarks that her husband's "phase" is no longer fashionable, and decides that he must die as a result of this one-too-many queer "relapse"; the man's dog laps up some of the spilled blood before chasing Luke out the front door. Immediately thereafter, Luke's well-being is endangered yet again by the "three stooges," a trio of baseball-bat-wielding gaybashers who look forward to rearranging his face and making him swallow his own teeth; their plan is foiled, however, when Luke pulls out a gun (which he stole earlier from the serial-killing lesbians) and shoots all three of the bashers dead in their tracks. As he flees from that encounter, Luke flags down Jon's car and lands on its hood, bringing together the two HIV-infected individuals and uniting their futures.

During their first sexual encounter back at Jon's apartment, about an hour after their destinies collide, as Jon worries about the safety of his wallet and CD collection as well as how to tell Luke about their (potential) need to engage in safe sex, Luke allays both of his fears by pointing out that Jon is a bit too paranoid and by welcoming him to the (AIDS) club. This exchange occurs just seconds after Luke drops his pants in front of Jon to take a shower but then changes his mind, finds the bare-chested Jon in the bedroom, pins him down on the bed, and runs his finger seductively down Jon's torso from his Adam's apple to his waist.

Once they begin spending time together, and immediately following their first night of sex, Luke explains to Jon the liberating aspects of their both being HIV-positive at a time when that health status appeared inevitably to lead to a rapid demise. Over their breakfast meal of miniature donuts and Barbie cereal with beer, Luke expresses that they, and others like them, are victims of the sexual revolution, of the generation before them that got to have all of the fun and has left them with the life-threatening tab. "Anybody who got fucked before safe sex *is* fucked," Luke explains. "I think it's all a part of the neo-Nazi Republican final solution. Germ warfare, you know? Genocide." This exchange explains what Luke meant the preceding day when he wrote the words "I Blame Society" in Magic Marker on a parking-garage pillar. Accordingly, Luke reasons that he and Jon, as individuals with finite futures, have nothing to lose, so they can say, "Fuck work, fuck the system, fuck everything" and do whatever they so desire. As an example, Luke whips out a credit card that he "borrowed" from his "uncle" and the two set out to indulge in an afternoon of unbridled purchasing, with the goal of maxing out the card's entire credit line.

It is during this illicit shopping spree that the pair encounter a neo-Nazi punk, unintentionally offended by Jon and Luke's quick kiss on the side-walk, who then intentionally offends them by explaining that AIDS actually stands for "Adios, infected dick suckers" (as discussed at the start of chapter 1). Although Jon wishes to walk away from the heated confrontation and pretend like nothing has happened, Luke has a very different reaction—he chases the punk down the street and beats him over the head repeatedly with one of their new purchases, a boom box, killing him. It is at this moment that Jon more fully glimpses the true nature of the individual with whom he has become so intimately involved so quickly, and what he discovers scares him. Fleeing to Jon's apartment without any of their purchases in hand, Luke maintains that the punk deserved what he got, and that Jon also wanted to see the guy's head split open. Although that is very likely the case, Jon is visibly unable to accept such a reality and tells Luke that he needs to leave, raising his voice to a shout when Luke hesitates. Luke reluctantly departs, leading Jon to commiserate with Darcy at a late-night diner about his de-structive attraction to psychopaths and the fact that he simply can't get Luke—the way he smells, how it feels to touch him—out of his head. Jon concludes that he is either extremely needy at the moment or else extremely horny.

Luke refuses to stay away for long, and the killing of the neo-Nazi punk is by no means his last aggressive or murderous act. As Jon sleeps in bed that night, with the sounds of a nearby search helicopter filling his room, a dark shadow moves across his face and he stirs, awakening to find Luke sit-ting on the mattress beside him, blood on his cheek and a loaded pistol in his mouth. Jon slowly pulls the pistol downward and comforts Luke with an embrace. Luke proceeds to explain, without providing any details at all about the circumstances of this unfortunate occurrence, that he believes he just killed a cop, and he begs Jon to help him get away. Clearly conflicted as to what he should do, Jon asks Luke why he should be the one to help him; Luke responds that Jon is the only person he knows. The helicopter sounds grow closer and intensify; the duo make off into the night.

Initially, Jon and Luke are headed to San Francisco, where Luke claims he has a friend they can stay with for a while, contradicting what he has just said to Jon. Upon their arrival at the man's home, however, it turns out that he is someone Luke claims to have spent the night with a few years earlier following a gay-pride parade who does not recall that encounter; he slams the door in Luke's face. This leads the duo to simply drive toward an unknown destination, taking them on an unintended cross-country odyssey. Along the way, Luke's violent tendencies reveal themselves several more times. When Jon returns from washing up at a rest area, he finds, to his dismay, Luke lying on the top of their car, wielding his "security blanket"—his pistol—in broad daylight, despite Jon's requests that he be more discreet with it. (During this incident, Luke suggests that they drive to Washington, D.C. and "blow Bush's brains out—or, better yet, we can hold him at gunpoint [and] inject him with a syringeful of our blood" in order to motivate the discovery of an immediate cure for AIDS.) Later, when a man accosts them in a supermarket parking lot at night, Luke instantly aims the gun at the nocturnal wanderer to make him go away. After Jon gets a parking ticket that pisses him off, Luke pulls out the gun with the intention of shooting the offending parking cop as they drive by. After Luke becomes angered by an out-of-order ATM, he returns to the car, grabs the pistol, and shoots the machine five times, causing its alarm to sound. When Jon reaches his violence-tolerance breaking point shortly thereafter, upon discovering that Luke has slit one of his own wrists in order to examine his HIV-infected blood, and declares that their vacation in the sun is now over, Luke points the gun menacingly in Jon's face, fires it just to the left of Jon's head, and, following a brief struggle between the two, uses the gun to hit Jon in the head and knock him unconscious.

As these various plot developments reveal, *The Living End* is, in both its style and storyline, a somewhat angry, in-your-face, confrontational film. Araki, who wrote the original draft of the screenplay in 1988, says that it came "from a very dark, personal place" ("Production" 7). With regard to this point, he elaborates:

> Those feelings of dread and insecurity which characterized the mid-late '80s AIDS crisis pervaded the consciousness of my whole generation. Even though I am HIV-negative, the specter of the virus loomed overhead like a radioactive cloud. Suddenly, sex, love, trust, desire—which are troublesome enough in themselves for gays *and* straights—were even more emotionally treacherous. What *would* I do if I tested positive? How would I

feel? What would my reaction be? Being something of a hopeless romantic, I found the concept of "till death do us part" more and more thematically and metaphorically pertinent. (Araki, "Production" 7)

Perhaps this serves to explain why, in addition to being so angry and confrontational, the film is simultaneously so incredibly hot and sexy, such as
when Luke gives Jon a blowjob beneath the steering wheel while the pair
drive past police on the side of the road, Jon and Luke engage in bareback
sex in the shower, Luke successfully persuades Jon to choke him as he begins to come, or the camera simply lingers a bit too long on one or both of
their fully exposed, sinewy torsos. Araki has said that he has always viewed
The Living End as "a love story calling for tolerance and compassion"
("Production" 7), and that aspect of the film certainly shines through, in addition to its social commentary pertaining to HIV/AIDS and the treatment of
non-heterosexual individuals and people with AIDS. The work was intended
to operate on different levels, in part as an expression of the despair, uncer-
tainty, and "seize-the-day urgency" of life in the age of AIDS, and in part as
a universal story about the disruptive and all-consuming nature of love and
the consequences that sometimes accompany it (Araki, "Filmmaker's" 4).

   At the start of *The Living End*, prior to any opening credits or the film's
title, on-screen text identifies this work as "an irresponsible movie by Gregg
Araki." After viewing the film in its entirety, the typical viewer likely concludes that this label pertains to numerous socially irresponsible aspects of
the film's content, such as the bareback sex that Jon and Luke engage in
during the age of AIDS, Jon consenting to choke Luke while they are having
sex, the blowjob Jon receives while driving, Luke's driving without a license
and swigging Jack Daniel's as he does so, the duo's L.A. shopping spree
using a stolen credit card, repeated instances of public urination, Luke's decision to kill himself as soon as he experiences his first visible HIV/AIDS
symptom, Luke's continual use of violence as a means of expressing his
frustration, and/or Jon's apparent decision to remain with a psychopathic
boyfriend at the film's end. The U.S. government's indifferent response to
the AIDS crisis represents yet another type of irresponsibility addressed in
the film, and it is reinforced at the end of the closing credits with Araki's
dedication of the film to Craig Lee, a seminal figure in the L.A. punk scene
with a small role in the film who passed away prior to its release and was the
first person Araki knew personally who died of AIDS, as well as to "the
hundreds of thousands who've died and the hundreds of thousands more
who will die because of a big white house full of Republican fuckheads."
There is a bit more than this to the "irresponsible movie" label at the film's
beginning, however.

According to Araki, the phrase "irresponsible movie" comes from a scholarly essay he read while in film school, by film theorist Robin Wood, about the classic 1938 screwball comedy *Bringing Up Baby* (directed by Howard Hawks), which stars Katharine Hepburn as a fun-loving, baby-leopard-owning socialite who teaches the more uptight object of her affections, a repressed paleontologist played by Cary Grant, to lighten up and begin to enjoy life more fully. In other words, as Araki explains in *The Living End*'s DVD commentary, the reckless and wild free spirit in *Bringing Up Baby* ends up destroying the paleontologist's everyday life as he has come to know it in order to set him free, thereby liberating him from his shortsightedness and repression.

Screwball comedy is a cinematic subgenre that Araki, as a film student in the 1980s, was exposed to regularly, and it is one that he intentionally strived to incorporate, in queer ways, within *The Living End*. Screwball comedy was especially popular during the mid 1930s and early 1940s as a means of getting around some of the repressive restrictions of the Motion Picture Production Code, which prohibited various topics and phenomena, such as homosexuality, adultery, and overt sexual activity, from explicitly being portrayed on-screen. As a result, the writers and directors of these comedies regularly utilized rapid-fire dialogue and innuendo to stand in for the sexual tension evident between their protagonists that was unable to come to fruition blatantly on-screen, in ways that would evade the attention of film censors, with audience members learning to read between the lines to determine the various sexual developments that likely occurred between such characters. The resulting sexual tension was then frequently sublimated into a battle of the sexes, accomplished primarily through carefully chosen words, glances, and gestures, that presented distinct opportunities for more liberated gender and class roles, with female characters typically dominating their surrounding males and the apparent antagonism existing between them ultimately resulting in romance. As such, the creation of desire among characters that may seem initially to be mismatched, and the resulting construction of romance between them despite the numerous obstacles they must overcome, are two of the primary attributes of screwball comedies (Shumway 390). In addition, the contents of screwball comedies regularly embody noteworthy political and social concerns of their historical eras (Belton 155).

Araki's decision to incorporate noteworthy aspects of screwball comedy in *The Living End*, therefore, makes sense, as his queering of this subgenre allows him to transform its traditional focus on liberation and gender into a new focus on liberation and sexual orientation in an offering that explores the obstacle-filled construction of romance between seemingly mismatched protagonists amid the backdrop of the AIDS pandemic, certainly one of the most noteworthy political and social concerns of the era in which the film was made and released. "The structure of [*Bringing Up Baby*] is kind of the same as *The Living End* in that it was about this spirited, free-willed character who frees this repressed, more normal-life character" (D. Smith, par. 5), the director has stated. It is perhaps entirely unsurprising, therefore, that Jon becomes "corrupted" by Luke, or at the very least begins acting more and more like him as his defenses weaken, over the course of Araki's film, such as when Jon refuses to "fondle [Luke's] crotch" one day while he is driving, on the grounds that he is a "responsible driver," but then readily accepts a blowjob from Luke while he is driving shortly thereafter, or when Jon finally resorts to violence himself—first by pounding Luke repeatedly in the chest during a heated argument, and later by striking Luke across the face quite forcefully after he finds that Luke has slit his own wrist—as a means of expressing his own frustration. This resulting state of affairs also serves to explain why Jon (apparently) decides to stay with Luke at the end of the film, despite all of his competing reservations and the violence that has been directed against him, because his everyday life as he had come to know it (pre-HIV-infection and pre-Luke) now ceases to exist and he, like Luke, has been set free, liberated (by HIV/AIDS) from his previous shortsightedness and repressed way of being.

Politically Progressive Attributes and Representational Strengths

As a leading example of the New Queer Cinema, *The Living End* is impressive for a variety of reasons, not the least of which is that is was made, guerilla-style without location permits and by a skeletal crew, on a budget of approximately twenty thousand dollars, with Araki serving as the film's writer, director, camera operator, and editor. It is perhaps even more impressive, however, for its daring, unconventional representations of gay male sexuality and people with HIV/AIDS.

Given the media-influenced socially constructed environment within which AIDS seized the anxious American imagination in the early to mid 1980s, it is not entirely surprising that the stigma of AIDS had become inextricably linked to the stigma of homosexuality by the time that the New Queer Cinema emerged, or that New Queer Cinema offerings addressing the AIDS pandemic directly typically featured gay men as their protagonists (Clark 9). Although the repeated reliance on representing gay men as the primary individuals with HIV/AIDS in such films served, deleteriously, to perpetuate widely shared, inaccurate cultural notions of AIDS as a "gay disease" or "gay plague," it nevertheless simultaneously provided opportunities for a larger number of gay male characters to appear on U.S. cinema screens than in the past, thereby offering "significant possibilities for altering and expanding the commonly accepted ways by which non-gays perceive and discuss the status of gay men and their lived realities" (Hart, *AIDS* 49) in contemporary U.S. society and contributing potentially quite meaningfully to "the 'coming out' of the gay community [by] . . . tear[ing] away the curtain of invisibility that had hitherto enveloped it" (Padgug and Oppenheimer 251).

In contrast to the majority of AIDS-themed movies that were targeted to mainstream audiences during the 1980s and 1990s, which typically offer only a kid-gloves representation of gay male sexuality (if any overt representation of it at all), Araki's *The Living End*, like other independent theatrical releases created under the guidance of queer directors and/or targeted substantially to queer audiences, provides a much more realistic, well-rounded portrayal of the lived social and sexual realities of gay men in contemporary U.S. society. Whereas NBC's broadcast standards department was so concerned about including anything that could be regarded as condoning homosexuality in its made-for-television AIDS movie *An Early Frost* (John Erman, 1985) that the offering does nothing at all from a representational standpoint to suggest that gay lovers Michael (played by Aidan Quinn) and Peter (played by D.W. Moffett) are actually anything more than roommates or best friends (Farber 23; Watney 112-13), and Hollywood's first all-star movie about AIDS, *Philadelphia* (1993, Jonathan Demme), does little (beyond having the central gay couple slow dance together at a costume party alongside a married straight couple) to suggest that Andrew Beckett (played by Tom Hanks) and Miguel Alvarez (played by Antonio Banderas) are actually sexually involved life partners rather than simply close friends, such squeamish treatment of gay male sexuality is lacking entirely in *The Living End*.

In its place, the viewer is presented with a series of sexually charged, potentially shocking images of Luke pleasuring a john by beating him on his bare ass with a tennis racquet, Luke seducing Jon with some assistance from his bottle of Jack Daniel's, Jon and Luke kissing very passionately, the two having sex along the roadside in the back seat of Jon's car, Luke rubbing his naked body repeatedly against Jon's in bed at the Paradise Motel, and Jon barebacking Luke in the shower and agreeing to choke his companion when Luke starts to come, in addition to the aforementioned blowjob beneath the steering wheel as Jon drives past the police. Through all of these encounters, the camera lingers on and fetishizes the bodies of these men, emphasizing their smoldering sexuality—an incredibly appealing yet atypical way of representing gay male characters who are HIV-positive on-screen, and one that has been referred to as a "gay porn pastiche" by at least one critic, who points out that Araki foregrounds the iconography of contemporary gay male porn in this film (Grundmann 26-27). The viewer is also presented with a series of touching, romantic moments between the two gay protagonists, such as when Luke draws a huge heart on the window of the phone booth in which Jon is talking to Darcy and writes "Jon + Luke, till death do us part" in the middle of it, or when Luke tells Jon that he is wild about him, or when Luke playfully moons Jon repeatedly outdoors in order to get Jon off the phone.

Another representational strength of *The Living End* is that it rejects the notion that gay men in the age of AIDS must either conform to engaging in only the most sterile forms of safe sex or else relinquish all sexual desire. Early in the film, shortly after he has learned that he is HIV-positive and is lying bare-chested on his bed, listening to his audio journal, Jon receives a telephone call out of the blue, from a man who wants to know if he is ready to get off. Not recognizing the man's voice, Jon is at first shocked, but he soon becomes a bit amused, believing the call to be a joke, when the man tells him that he got Jon's number from a telephone bulletin board and asks what he looks like. "Are you hard? What are you wearing? How big is your cock?" the man inquires as Jon responds that he has to go, and that such information is none of the man's business. He hangs up the phone, bemused. Undeterred, the man calls again the next day, after Jon has just spent the night with Luke and then banned him from his apartment as a result of his killing the neo-Nazi punk. When he asks if Jon is ready to get off, Jon angrily dismisses his invitation, slamming down the phone's receiver. At a time when HIV/AIDS was spreading rapidly, phone sex represented one of the safest (albeit simultaneously one of the most sterile) forms of safe sex. By having Jon choose to reject this sexual option, the film representationally suggests that gay male sexual desire in the age of AIDS, even among HIV-positive individuals, does not need to be reduced to such clinical forms of expression, nor does it have to be repressed entirely. Luke reinforces this same point explicitly in dialogue, during a heated moment, when he asks Jon, "You really want to go back to your 'I'm HIV-positive and everything's normal, hunky-dory' life? Well, go fuckin' right ahead. Just don't forget to have sex in a plastic bag. . . . I say fuck that shit, man."

Yet another representational strength of *The Living End* is that it plays with established (sub)genre conventions in order to defy death in relation to HIV/AIDS. As an example of the road movie subgenre, which has been utilized in all sorts of films to date ranging from screwball comedies to horror films and films noir, Araki's film features protagonists who experience both the freedom and challenges of life in unfamiliar terrain and the newfound knowledge, personal awakening, and/or tragedy that typically results (Johnson, par. 1, 3). Like the characters Wyatt/Captain America (played by Peter Fonda) and Billy (played by Dennis Hopper) in *Easy Rider* (Dennis

Hopper, 1969), an influential film that removed women from the road trip altogether, Jon and Luke discover the various rifts that exist between the dominant culture and its various subcultures, as well as national discourses pertaining to tradition and transition, in their particular historical era as they travel America's back roads (Cohan and Hark 9; Klinger 179, 199). More specifically, however, Araki explains in his DVD commentary that he made *The Living End* in the tradition of couple-on-the-run movies such as *Bonnie and Clyde* (Arthur Penn, 1967), *Gun Crazy* (Joseph H. Lewis, 1949), and *They Live by Night* (Nicholas Ray, 1949), works that feature outlaw couples on the lam in out-of-control, hostile universes that appear intent on destroying them. The characters in these films endeavor to overcome restrictive constraints of time and place as well as powerful feelings of rage and disempowerment (Leong, Sell, and Thomas 73, 78). They also experience contradictions pertaining to domesticity, mobility, and desire while simultaneously challenging traditional conceptions of taste and proper behavior (Leong, Sell, and Thomas 85). Araki's film has also frequently been referred to by critics as a "gay" *Thelma and Louise* (Ridley Scott, 1991), the film released a year prior to *The Living End* which stars Geena Davis and Susan Sarandon as best friends who hit the road, without any specific destination, to escape from the monotony of their daily lives and unexpectedly become outlaws (Hays, *View* 39; Kaufman 19). Given longstanding genre expectations, the presumed ending of these sorts of films is that one or more of the characters on the lam will be killed in the film's climax, with the road ultimately serving as a big dead end. Death of one or more protagonists is also the expected ending of many movies pertaining to HIV/AIDS, especially those that were made and released during the pandemic's first decade.

As a result, given the film's storyline and the HIV-positive status of its protagonists, the presumed ending of a film like *The Living End* would be that either Jon or Luke—or both of them—will perish on-screen before the closing credits begin to roll. Such an expectation is further promoted in the film itself by its repeated incorporation of attributes pertaining to death. For example, the bumper sticker on Jon's car when the viewer first meets him reads "Choose Death." The compact disc that Jon purchases prior to learning of his HIV status is by the band Dead Can Dance. The article that Jon is working on at the time he meets Luke pertains to the death of cinema. Darcy, when checking on Jon's apartment, finds his goldfish outside of its bowl, dead on the floor. While they are having sex, Luke asks Jon if he would prefer to die for sex or for love. While lounging poolside with Luke, Jon discovers that the batteries in his voice recorder are dead. Luke mentions that his mother died when he was only three years old after she was hit by a garbage truck, and that he once saw a bag lady jump off the top of a skyscraper to her death, shattering every bone in her body. He also mentions that he plans to "off himself" the moment he notices his first symptom of HIV/AIDS, and that he would prefer to die while having an orgasm. In addition, toward the end of the film, Jon says that he regards Luke as a vampire who is sucking the life force out of him. From a representational standpoint, therefore, it is particularly noteworthy that the viewer's generic expectation pertaining to death remains unfulfilled. Instead, the otherwise ambiguous ending of the film, with these "outlaws" alone together on the beach at sunset, makes it clear that the lives of these two characters will continue to go on. Theirs is, paradoxically, a "living" end, one that offers hope to people with HIV/AIDS everywhere that, at least in fantasy (if not yet in reality at the time of the film's release), this medical condition can be outrun and outlived and that life for all can go on.

In summing up the various representational strengths of this noteworthy and intriguing film, Roy Grundmann has written:

> *The Living End* speaks to a generation tired of rehearsing safe-sex practices like a flight attendant demonstrating safety procedures before takeoff. As a fantasy, the film is about emotions and desire; as a political project, it demonstrates that this desire does not exist in a totally separate, devious subculture but has historically been fed by and always expressed in relation to mainstream culture. . . . [N]o matter which [protagonist] the spectator identifies with or desires, he/she always ends up in an HIV-positive position. . . . Luke infects Jon like a virus, and we are infected along with him. As infection blurs with infatuation, disease becomes a metaphor for accumulating rage and impetus for social change. (26-27)

Stereotypes, (Potential) Misogyny, and Representational Shortcomings

Despite the noteworthy representational strengths of *The Living End*, the film simultaneously contains some equally noteworthy representational shortcomings that detract from its overall appeal. Throughout cinema history, there has been a recurring over-reliance on representing non-heterosexual characters as psychopaths, murderers, and mentally unstable misfits (Bryant 60-61; Benshoff and Griffin 8-10; Russo 181-245). Although this has particularly been true in works geared primarily to mainstream audiences, offerings of the New Queer Cinema have similarly been accused of "recirculating negative stereotypes such as the queer psycho-killer" (Benshoff and Griffin 12). This is certainly the case with *The Living End*. For example, even though the character of Luke is intended to embody the anger and frustration associated with the AIDS crisis and to "show how social forces and/or sexual repression can and do cause violence" (Benshoff and

Griffin 12), the fact that he is yet another queer psychopath, rather than a more restrained sort of individual demonstrating less extreme reactions to the circumstances within which he finds himself, is nevertheless problematic from a representational standpoint. The same is true of the serial-killing lesbians in the red convertible bearing an "I love Jesus" bumper sticker, Daisy (played by Mary Woronov) and Fern (played by Johanna Went), who pick up the hitchhiking Luke at the start of the film. In that scene, the two women revel in belittling Luke by referring to him sarcastically as "a nomadic drifter," "a lonesome cowboy hitching across the country like Jack Kerouac," and an individual with only a "petite little taste of Vienna sausage" (to ensure that the viewer grasps that they are referring to a small penis, the women mention all of the following synonyms for that male appendage during this encounter: baloney pony, dingus, hotdog, love gun, pecker, peter, poker, prick, pussy plunger, smiling meat puppet, and wang). Aiming a gun at his face—which they vow to blow to smithereens—they also take pleasure in tormenting Luke with the possible ways they might kill him simply to get their kicks. Daisy informs Luke that the last guy Fern killed was shot in the "cock" but that she herself couldn't stand all of his bleeding, squealing, and whimpering during the twelve hours it took him to die. Prior to that, Fern shoved a huge ice pick up another guy's asshole in order to kill him, but that incident was a bit more tolerable because the man was bound and gagged, so he did not make quite as much noise. Fortunately for Luke, he is able to make a safe escape, stealing the convertible, when Fern steps out of the vehicle to urinate outdoors prior to murdering him and she screams (for some unknown reason), which motivates Daisy to run after her.

That representation of the serial-murdering Daisy and Fern is linked further to another representational shortcoming of *The Living End*: its negative representation of women in general. Like those two lesbian characters, the wife who walks in on her bisexual husband in bed resorts immediately to murderous tendencies. Apparently having promised the woman that he would swear off men for good, the husband admits to having had a "relapse" and apologizes for his indiscretion. Nevertheless, feeling that she can no longer forgive his behavior and appearing quite emotionally fragile, the wife readily removes a huge kitchen knife from the purse she is carrying and stabs her husband with it, killing him.

Just when it seems that the representation of women in the film cannot get much less flattering, things take yet another turn for the worse. For despite those extreme plot developments involving its female characters, the most negative representation of women in *The Living End* actually occurs with regard to the character of Darcy, Jon's obsessively devoted fag-hag friend.

When Jon first visits Darcy, an artist and painter, to inform her of the distressing medical news he has received, she appears to be in shock, embracing him tightly and verbally expressing her disbelief. As their exchange continues, Darcy refuses to release Jon entirely from her hold, and she strokes his chest repeatedly to comfort him, fulfilling a physically and psychologically nurturing role. She reassures him that she will always be there for him, whenever he needs her. Never has a more true statement been uttered on film. Despite the fact that she has a live-in boyfriend, Peter (played by Scot Goetz), who feels increasingly ignored and neglected, Darcy begins to spend her every waking moment obsessing about Jon and his health status, especially once he is on the road with Luke and can only contact her occasionally, consistently reversing the charges, by telephone.

After Jon kicks Luke out of his apartment in the wake of the (likely) neo-Nazi punk killing, Darcy rushes to meet and comfort him at a late-night restaurant. Afterward, as they prepare to go their separate ways, Darcy invites Jon to sleep over at her place (even though her boyfriend is there) so that they can talk all night and go out for breakfast together in the morning, and she asks if he blames her for worrying about him. Jon's reply suggests that even *he* feels her caring is becoming a bit overbearing: "Darce, really, it's getting to be like 'rally around the fag.'" Nonetheless, his words do not deter her. She merely tousles his hair affectionately and reluctantly returns home alone, where she discovers Peter waiting up for her and announces that she likely won't be able to sleep again that night. Sexily clad in a nightshirt with black underwear beneath it, Peter follows Darcy to the kitchen and asks if she wants to have sex. She responds that she is far too worried about Jon because he has never seemed so lost before, which causes Peter to sigh. Peter then attempts a second time, in vain, to persuade Darcy to go to bed with him.

Darcy's simultaneous obsession with Jon and neglect of Peter only intensifies from there. When Jon calls her for the first time from the road, it is clear that Darcy's endless concern for him has resulted in artist's block—as her telephone begins to ring, she is shown staring blankly at the canvas in front of her, upon which she is trying unsuccessfully to paint. Hearing Jon's voice on the line, however, perks her back up instantly. Although Jon announces that he can't talk for long, he takes a few moments to inform Darcy that he and Luke are in a "shitload of trouble," that he has certainly "bitten off more than [he] can gag on, that's for sure," and that he needs her to attend to several errands for him: call his editor and get him a deadline extension on his death-of-cinema article, pay his rent (which was due last week), bring in his mail, and feed his goldfish. He hangs up abruptly to be with Luke, who is attempting to pry Jon's hands from the receiver. Naturally, given her extreme level of devotion to Jon, Darcy drops everything and rushes directly over to his apartment, where she carries in his mail, listens to his answering-machine messages, waters his plants, and even discards a plateful of old food that he was snacking on before he departed. By the time Jon calls again the next day, Darcy has already been reduced to a torpid individual who appears capable only of smoking while sitting next to her telephone. She tells him that she has been worried sick about him, to the extent that she has been unable to eat or sleep, her face has broken out, and she is driving Peter crazy. Jon implores Darcy to stop worrying about him. "The whole world's spiraling out of control," she melodramatically concludes, as Jon promises to call again in a few days.

Not hearing from Jon more frequently takes a very heavy toll on Darcy. She once again rejects Peter sexually—this time pushing him off of her body in bed—because she has too many things on her mind. "Unless you want me to lie here with my legs spread, taking it, can we just give it up already?" Darcy quips. Reminding her that it's been far too long since they've had sex, Peter insightfully tells Darcy that she needs to relax and stop letting a virus in somebody else's bloodstream ruin *her* life. "Jon is hardly what I would call 'somebody else,'" she snaps back. Darcy then apologizes to Peter for being such a "bitch" lately because Jon's circumstances have her so "fucked up," but her words fall on deaf ears. Peter informs Darcy that he has started seeing someone else; Darcy gives him two minutes to pack up his things and get out.

With Peter out of her life, apparently for good, Darcy devotes her every waking moment to obsessing further about her HIV-positive gay friend. With the telephone right beside her, she spends her day sitting on the stairs in her apartment, smoking cigarettes, drinking Diet Coke, and playing with a mechanical toy fish that, when she claps her hands loudly, flops around and falls down to the step below. Finding herself in need of more cigarettes, she reluctantly steps away from the phone to rush out and buy some. Upon her return, she finds that her telephone is ringing. Although she stumbles up the indoor staircase frantically, she does not answer it in time, and she concludes that she has just missed the latest call from Jon (which, the viewer learns, is indeed the case). At this moment, Darcy has reached her breaking point. She slams down the receiver and clutches the telephone to her bosom, gasping and sighing, on the verge of tears. She then carries the telephone with her downstairs, places it on the floor, and squats down beside it, visibly distraught; the camera shoots downward at her from an extremely high angle in order to emphasize her extreme sense of isolation and emotional desperation. Twenty seconds later, she picks up a huge box filled with Styrofoam packing peanuts, crashes it down repeatedly upon a nearby designer's mannequin, and collapses to the floor, crying, burying her face in her hands. Although the rest of the world appears to be functioning quite regularly, it is certainly the case that, because of her unhealthy devotion to Jon, Darcy's whole world has indeed spiraled completely out of control. Her life only appears to regain a glint of purpose when the telephone starts to ring again seconds later and Jon informs her that he has decided to come home.

Clearly, from beginning to end in this film, Darcy is portrayed as an overly devoted fag hag who takes the nurturing maternal role that is expected by the heterosexist patriarchy to new extremes, with her telephone cord serving as Darcy's symbolic umbilical cord to Jon. As a result, she readily sacrifices happiness and success in her own professional and personal lives, as well as her own emotional needs, in order to devote all of her attention to caring for and about the (albeit gay) man whom she loves most deeply, further strengthening her devotion whenever Jon pushes her away, discouraging her clingy and smothering ways. This sort of retrograde representation, coupled with the negative representations of the other female characters in the film, in an otherwise groundbreaking work is both disconcerting and disappointing. Some critics have gone so far as to suggest that Araki's representations of women in *The Living End* are, in fact, misogynistic, but the director himself has refuted the veracity of such claims, explaining (on the DVD commentary track) that the work is neither anti-lesbian nor anti-female but rather intended to show how a positive HIV diagnosis affects, and has repercussions for, everyone who cares about the infected individual.

Despite their aforementioned noteworthy attributes, Araki's representations of the gay male protagonists in *The Living End* are simultaneously somewhat problematic, as well. From the boyfriend in *An Early Frost* who conceals the fact that he regularly trolls local gay bars and bathhouses to have unprotected sex with promiscuous men because his partner has become too busy with work to immediately gratify his sexual needs to the gay male members of the self-proclaimed gang of "raging, atheist, meat-eating, HIV-positive terrorists" in *Chocolate Babies* (Stephen Winter, 1996) who enjoy barebacking on a regular basis as well as cutting their hands and smearing inflected blood on politicians whom they feel are not doing enough to assist people with AIDS, one of the most common representations of gay men in fictional movies addressing the AIDS pandemic to date has involved portraying them as sexually promiscuous individuals who irresponsibly endanger the health and well-being of their surrounding others, either by placing them at increased risk of contracting HIV/AIDS or by endangering them in sexually violent or aggressive ways (Hart, *AIDS* 52). Whenever this occurs, it harmfully reinforces the stereotype, so widely shared in U.S. society from the advent of the AIDS pandemic, that gay men are somehow "guilty villains" in the AIDS crisis, in dramatic contrast to the pandemic's so-called "innocent victims" (such as blood-transfusion recipients and infants born to

infected mothers) or its "relatively innocent victims" (generally monogamous, relatively non-promiscuous heterosexuals who nevertheless contract
HIV/AIDS as a result of "non-deviant" forms of heterosexual sexual activity) (Hart, *AIDS* 40). In a subtle way, Araki perpetuates this sort of deleterious stereotype in *The Living End* by showing the HIV-positive Luke engaging in kinky, (apparently) unprotected sex with the bisexual john who picks
him up on the side of an L.A. roadway and then seducing Jon just a few
hours later, after the hustler-drifter abandons his plan to take a shower in
between those sexual encounters (Hart, *AIDS* 52). Far more blatantly, however, the director perpetuates the stereotype of queer villainy by having Luke
rape Jon during the film's powerful yet extremely disturbing concluding sequence, in addition to all of the other increasingly violent acts he has carried
out over the course of the film's narrative.

During this concluding encounter, after Luke has knocked Jon unconscious with his pistol to prevent him from leaving, Luke licks some of Jon's
infected blood from the side of his head and then drags Jon's shirtless body
toward the car. When Jon comes to, coughing, he finds that he and Luke are
on a deserted beach; Luke has already bound his wrists behind him and is
beginning to undress him. When Jon asks what he is doing, Luke climbs
atop Jon, pushing his back to the ground, and, with his lips just inches away
from Jon's, responds intensely, "Can't you see? I love you more than life."
Jon declares that Luke is crazy; Luke pulls down Jon's jeans and underwear,
takes out his own penis, spits in his hand to provide a bit of lubrication, pulls
the pistol from his pocket and cocks it in his own mouth, and then initiates
his sexual assault. Jon's clenched eyes and lips register the pain he is experiencing as Luke repeatedly thrusts into him, increasing the tempo as the rape
progresses. As Luke approaches his climax, Jon defiantly and repeatedly
commands him to pull the trigger so that Luke can have the "ultimate orgasm" he has been desiring for so long and Jon can be done with him, once
and for all. When Luke actually pulls the trigger, however, the pistol does
not fire, because it is out of bullets. This unexpected development motivates
the disappointed Luke to remove the gun from his mouth, sit up, throw the
gun away forcefully in the direction of the ocean, and untie Jon's hands. Jon
immediately pulls his pants and underwear back up, sits up, links eyes with
Luke for several seconds—and punches Luke hard in the face. He then rises,
buttons his jeans, and walks off, leaving Luke alone on the beach with the
sound of its loudly crashing waves. This, I believe, is where many first-time
viewers of the film believe the story is ending. Twenty seconds later, however, Jon slowly returns, hesitates, and plops down in the sand beside Luke,
looking emotionally and physically drained. He takes Luke's arm in his
hands and rests his head on Luke's leather-jacketed shoulder. They sit there,
together alone, in silence at sunset.

About this concluding sequence, Araki himself has stated, "When Jon announces that he's had enough of living out a romantic fantasy and is returning home, he finds himself held at gunpoint, at the mercy of the unstable, unpredictable Luke. During an intense, sexual and emotional showdown on a deserted beach, their twisted relationship comes to an unnerving climax and an inevitable resolution" (Araki, "Synopsis" 5). After viewing it, an insightful viewer will likely conclude that the reason Jon returns to be with Luke at the film's end, despite having just been sexually violated by him, is that the world as he has known it now ceases to exist, so he does not know what else to do. From a representational standpoint, however, a more superficial reading of this closing sequence might suggest that Jon, as an HIV-positive gay male in the age of AIDS, must simply settle for whatever sort of close friendly or romantic companionship that he can get, even if it comes from a psychopath who has just raped him. In a world that tends to embrace victim-blaming strategies with regard to non-heterosexual individuals and "diabolical" diseases and pandemics, this latter sort of reading of the sequence is certainly socially and stereotypically troublesome. In dramatic contrast, even Jon's heterosexual, HIV-negative fag hag, Darcy, who presumably has many more companionship options according to this line of reasoning, had the good sense to tell her boyfriend to get lost—and simply because he had cheated on her.

Concluding Observations

Araki, as a self-described "film school brat," is proud of his extensive knowledge of cinematic (sub)genres and auteurs, and he regularly combines various aspects of them in his own creations, typically defying genre expectations by utilizing such elements in unique ways to communicate unexpected ideological messages and putting a queer spin on them in the process (D'Arcy, par. 49). For example, in *The Living End*, Araki's incorporation and subsequent intentional rejection of the trope of sterile safe sex from numerous AIDS movies ends up producing a unique representation of gay male sexual expression in the age of AIDS, even among HIV-positive individuals. In addition, Araki's incorporation of noteworthy aspects of couple-on-the-run road movies and subsequent rejection of the presumed ending of those sorts of films ends up offering hope to individuals with HIV/AIDS that their medical condition may ultimately be outrun, rather than resulting in near-certain death. As such, the director's commitment to genre in *The Living End* works effectively to produce several of his radical film's most noteworthy representational strengths.

At the same time, however, Araki's penchant for referencing well-known films and (sub)genres simultaneously serves as a stumbling block that produces several of his film's representational shortcomings. His problematic representations of the murderous Luke and the serial-killing lesbians he encounters early in *The Living End*, for example, are clearly inspired by the representations found commonly in the grindhouse films of the late 1960s and 1970s. These types of exploitation films, named after the kinds of theaters in which they typically were shown (former burlesque theaters that historically featured "bump and grind" dancing), regularly explored cultural taboos by featuring suggestive or explicit sexual acts, bizarre acts of visceral violence, blood and gore, and over-the-top instances of mayhem and rebellion in works that eschewed traditional conceptions of artistic merit and quality. Although such films were readily dismissed by most critics during their heyday, they have since been acknowledged as containing solid doses of social and political commentary, even if many of their viewers failed to notice. Daisy and Fern in Araki's film are clearly a contemporary version of the murderous sports-car-driving go-go dancers who serve as the central characters of the grindhouse classic *Faster, Pussycat! Kill! Kill!* (Russ Meyer, 1965), individuals who thrive on the thrills provided by sex, violence, speed, and power, and Luke is a contemporary male version of them (Stringer 176).

By incorporating these types of characters in order to produce a more titillating viewing experience, however, Araki inadvertently and problematically perpetuates the longstanding cinematic stereotype of queer psychopaths, a reality that is all the more troubling in a historical era during which anti-queer sentiment was on the rise as a result of the AIDS pandemic. Similarly, by incorporating and queering noteworthy aspects of screwball comedy in order to transform the subgenre's traditional focus on liberation and gender into a new focus on liberation and sexual orientation in *The Living End*, Araki ends up producing a representation, if analyzed superficially, of a young, gay, HIV-positive man who is forced to settle for whatever sort of romantic and sexual companionship he can find—even if it is provided by another HIV-positive man who has sexually violated him—as these seemingly mismatched protagonists and the apparent antagonism that exists between them ultimately results in romance, despite the numerous obstacles (including rape) that they encounter along the way. As such, Araki's vision of what it meant to be a filmmaker in the early 1990s, at a time when he was endeavoring to make provocative films pertaining to non-heterosexuality and HIV/AIDS by regularly referencing well-known works created by the various auteurs who came before him and engaging in generic hybridization with a queer twist, was both a blessing and a curse when it came to creating

the New Queer Cinema offering that launched him to international prominence.

With this groundbreaking film, Araki has created, despite its representational shortcomings, an important offering of the New Queer Cinema that
powerfully communicates the anger and frustration experienced by gay men
and others during the first decade of the AIDS crisis (and beyond). "It was
raw and provocative and challenging, and it really pushed people's buttons,"
the director has stated, in response to an interviewer's characterization of the
film as being "angry, it was punk rock, it was 'Fuck you, I'm gay. Fuck your
world'" (D. Smith, par. 8-9). "People were getting so passionate and crazy,
which to me as a filmmaker was exciting, that something I had done created
such a strong response" (D. Smith, par. 9), Araki continued. "[W]hen we
started making this movie, it was just this little tiny art project, [one that ul-
timately] . . . created this sort of global stir that we never really anticipated.
So it was kind of an amazing experience" (D. Smith, par. 9).

What is evident from this film is that a truly unique, innovative, and
boundary-pushing director was emerging on the international scene in relation to the New Queer Cinema phenomenon. Perhaps even more importantly, Araki's trademark in-your-face style as an auteur director was also
beginning to crystallize, one possessing a confrontational aesthetic that
regularly reworks established film (sub)genres—such as the couple-on-the-
run movie, the road movie, and even the juvenile delinquency movie—in
queer ways, most notably by festishizing the bodies and erotically charged
interactions of non-heterosexual characters; exploring shocking, frequently
taboo subject matter and romantic and sexual scenarios on-screen; serving
up plenty of extreme(ly) sexual and/or violent images; trapping alienated,
conflicted, and/or isolated characters tightly within the confines of the
frame; favoring somewhat lengthy scenes that play out in real time; giving
voice to marginalized members of the LGBTQ community and its various
subgroups; demonstrating an intentional lack of traditional commercial appeal; and refusing to take each film and its subject matter entirely seriously.
With regard to this style, which he has described as containing an "outsider
sensibility" (D. Smith, par. 17), Araki has proudly stated that his "movies on
homosexuality and bisexuality can turn straight men into gays because of
their eroticism" (Ehrenstein 70) and that he "couldn't make movies like this
if [he] started to worry about what Jerry Falwell is going to have to say
about it" ("Biography," par. 10). In addition, the contents of *The Living End*
reveal the recurring attributes, approaches, and themes that Araki has continued to exploit throughout his entire body of cinematic work, which contribute so substantially to the successful execution of his style: alienated,
bored, nihilistic, rootless young people who are desperate to make meaningful connections with others; exploration of sexualities amid a cultural back-

drop of sex, drugs, and (post-punk/industrial) rock 'n' roll; complex roman-
tic/sexual pairings and love triangles; bizarre street people and other marginal characters who populate an at-times-surrealistic Los Angeles; and recurring elements of mise-en-scène including loudly decorated apartments,
endless freeways, claustrophobic mini-marts, gaudy motel rooms, and expansive parking lots.

In summing up his own breakthrough creation, Araki has described *The
Living End* as "an 'irresponsible' rant that was equal parts personal protest,
Godard-influenced art film, and couple-on-the-run genre romance," one that
inherently possesses "raw, rough-and-tumble 'guerilla' charm" and serves as
a "time capsule" of a time when AIDS was "robbing the world of an entire
generation" (Araki, "Spring" 2), "when people were dying every day all
around you and it felt like a war zone" (Duralde 65). He has also emphasized
that, with regard to positioning him as a leading director of the emergent
New Queer Cinema, such status was entirely unexpected, catching him entirely by surprise. "The impact and hubbub surrounding *The Living End* was
totally an accident. The film just happened to be in the right place at the
right time. It became the eye of this storm that no one expected," he has
noted (Hays, *View* 38).

Nevertheless, to the director's surprise and delight, *The Living End* had
garnered him international recognition at a time when he was still defining
himself as a distinctive director with a unique authorial style. At the end of
1992, during the height of his newfound cinematic notoriety, the directions
he would choose to go with his subsequent films remained anybody's guess.

Chapter 3
Refining an Authorial Style with *Totally F***ed Up* and *The Doom Generation*

In an L.A. apartment, a teenage lesbian is throwing a birthday party for her teenage partner, with whom she wishes to have a baby. The couple's four closest gay male friends are in attendance. One of the friends reads aloud from a personal ad placed by a "very oral butt-eater" who seeks a "face-sitter for regular sessions," as well as from an ad placed by a "horny, hairy top" who seeks a "slave/son/pet into B&D, . . . shaving, toys, enemas, water sports, [and] diapers," as a pot pipe is passed around. Another of the friends emerges from a back room, carrying a pornographic magazine and a condom filled with his ejaculate. He hands the used condom to one of the girls, who empties its contents into a large stainless steel bowl and, using a turkey baster, mixes it in with the rest of the bowl's contents. "You know mine are gonna swim the fastest," the boy says with confidence. The girls attempt to pressure another friend into contributing his sperm next, reminding him that everyone is expected to make a contribution, especially since they ate their snacks and drank their booze, but he insists that someone else go before him. Two of his companions oblige. An intertitle accompanying these on-screen developments reads, "It's my party and I'll inseminate if I want to."

The above scene appears in *Totally F***ed Up* (1993), Gregg Araki's follow-up release to *The Living End* and the first offering in what he has referred to as his "teen-apocalypse trilogy" ("Spring" 12). It demonstrates clearly how, with his next film, Araki continued intentionally to explore controversial, potentially taboo topics and offer provocative, potentially shocking images that had not previously been captured on film with any regularity, ones that are presented from an LGBTQ "insider" rather than an "outsider" point of view. In the aftermath of the media circus that nearly

33

consumed him following *The Living End*'s identification as an important offering, and he as a noteworthy director, of the emergent New Queer Cinema,
Araki set out next to create a series of three films that explore teen angst in
its numerous dimensions, with a continued emphasis on providing noteworthy representations of non-heterosexual individuals in a world that frequently treats them as outsiders. The subsequent offerings of the trilogy are
The Doom Generation (1995) and *Nowhere* (1997).

This chapter examines the first two films of Araki's teen-apocalypse
trilogy, *Totally F***ed Up* and *The Doom Generation*, with regard to how
they represent both noteworthy continuations of, and deviations from, the
emergent post-punk authorial style evident in the director's breakthrough
cinematic offering and the radical/subversive potential that is enabled by that
style. (For reasons that will gradually become evident, *Nowhere* is explored
at length in the next chapter of this project, along with Araki's 1999 film,
Splendor.) The discussion that follows is intended to demonstrate the process by which the director refined his trademark authorial style, which has its
roots in his earliest two feature-length films and began to crystallize more
completely in *The Living End*, through the process of creating his fourth and
fifth features.

Getting a Bit Too Heavy-handed with *Totally F***ed Up*

Once again, Araki served simultaneously as the writer, director, cinematographer, and editor of *Totally F***ed Up*, which follows the interconnected
actions and interactions of a close-knit, racially diverse group of six non-
heterosexual L.A. teens (four gay males and two lesbians) as they search for
happiness and meaning in their everyday existence. As they go about their
daily lives, occasionally smoking pot or taking Ecstasy to make them a bit
more bearable, they are frequently interviewed on videotape by Steven
(played by Gilbert Luna), the aspiring filmmaker in their group, who queries
them about various topics of relevance to being young and queer in the (at-
times-homophobic) big city as part of a documentary he is making. The
subjects of his interviews, in addition to himself (which he shoots holding
the camera in front of his face or with the assistance of a nearby tripod), are
Andy (played by James Duval), the brooding member of the group who
questions whether love actually exists, believes he might possibly be bisexual, and describes himself as being "totally fucked up," even though he
seems to have things pretty much together; Tommy (played by Roko Belic),
the promiscuous member of the group who is known to engage in a rapid series of anonymous sexual encounters, as if he were still living in the 1970s;

Deric (played by Lance May), an artist, and Steven's boyfriend until he learns of his partner's clandestine sexual encounters with another young man; and Michele and Patricia (played by Susan Behshid and Jenee Gill, respectively), the lesbian couple in the film that viewers get to know primarily as relatively indistinguishable individuals (aside from their differing physical statures and hair colors) who are remarkably like-minded and completely in love. Araki has summarized the overall contents and style of this film by stating that this "honest, open-structured look into the lives of gay/lesbian teens . . . explores the very serious problems confronting young homos today—AIDS, alienation, suicide, drugs, fagbashing violence, and not having a date on Saturday night" and is a "kinda twisted cross between avant-garde experimental cinema and a queer John Hughes flick" ("Totally" 6).

Araki's latter comment is particularly intriguing, given the range of content that this film unabashedly and unapologetically addresses about contemporary (queer) teen life that is lacking entirely from Hughes' films of a few years earlier, such as *Sixteen Candles* (1984), *The Breakfast Club* (1985), and *Ferris Bueller's Day Off* (1986). Accordingly, Araki once again is intentionally reworking the conventions of an established film subgenre—in this case, the teen movie—into queer scenarios, with queer characters decidedly in the forefront rather than on the margins, in order to utilize his outsider sensibility to give voice to the marginalized members of the teen community who are typically represented only minimally and stereotypically on film (if at all) and to create a powerful work pertaining to queer identity politics. About this topic, Araki has expressed:

> [T]he essential impetus behind the film was the desire to portray a way of life, a sub-subculture which is totally ignored by both the mainstream and the conventional gay media—to represent the unrepresented. I would venture to say that queer teenagers—with all their lovable confusions and complexities—have never before been depicted as they are in this movie. There is a tendency to sanitize, to gloss over, to moralize when dealing with the subject of young gays which I consciously avoided in the development of this project. ("Filmmaker's" 7)

In his attempts to distinguish this work still further from Hollywood's far more sanitized cinematic representations of contemporary teenagers, Araki intentionally cast actual teenagers to star in *Totally F***ed Up*, in dramatic contrast to the older actors who have typically been hired to play teenage characters in films such as *Fast Times at Ridgemont High* (Amy Heckerling, 1982) and *Heathers* (Michael Lehmann, 1989) (Araki, "Production" 8).

The realities of teenage life in the age of AIDS are presented clearly and candidly in *Totally F***ed Up*, perhaps most efficiently through the characters' videotaped interview responses which are intercut with the film's

narrative in a manner reminiscent of the highly influential, voyeuristic independent film *sex, lies, and videotape* (Steven Soderbergh, 1989). When
asked to share their personal views about sex, for example, Deric responds
that it tends to be overrated, Tommy says that it is an intense release akin to
a dam breaking, and Andy acknowledges that, while he is still trying to figure out what he likes, he finds "buttfucking" to be repulsive. (Pornographic
images of one man engaging in anal intercourse with another immediately
follow Andy's assessment, as Tommy and a blonde male teen he has just
met are shown masturbating together while viewing them.) When asked to
share his views about safe sex, Deric comments that it is better than in the
good old days, when guys were getting fisted in slings, having sex in the
bushes, and drinking each other's urine. (Images of him and Steven, naked
and fooling around in bed, follow this interview segment, along with a shot
of Michele and Patricia being intimate together in a bubble bath.) With regard to the topic of AIDS, Michele states that AIDS is biological warfare
and government-sponsored genocide, and Patricia notes that it is a
government-endorsed holocaust, both echoing the sentiments expressed
equally as blatantly in *The Living End*. (These remarks are immediately pre-
ceded by excerpts from a haunting "AIDS Kills" public service announce-
ment.) With regard to their (superficial) personal views about love, Michele
characterizes it as something to cling to other than television, Andy states
that it is a huge load of bullshit that individuals are trained to desire from
birth in fairytales, movies, pop songs, and lite-beer commercials, and
Tommy says that he falls in love constantly but it lasts only "as long as a
squirt in the dark." (These comments are followed by shots of the six friends
playing Heartthrob, a board game about heterosexual love, which they
spruce up by introducing queer scenarios to make it a bit more relevant and
interesting.) On the topic of their preferred euphemisms for masturbation,
Tommy reveals that he prefers the phrase "polishing the trophy," whereas
Deric prefers "stroking the dolphin," Andy prefers "shooting tadpoles at the
moon," Michele prefers "making oyster soup," and Patricia prefers "doing
the two-finger tango." (These interview excerpts immediately follow a sequence in which the four gay male teens discuss which presumably heterosexual male celebrities they prefer to jack off to, which include Matt Dillon,
Mel Gibson, and Tom Cruise, as well as graphic images of a large, erect
male penis being roughly manipulated by its possessor.)

The realities of teenage life in the age of AIDS are also communicated
clearly through the film's narrative developments, which focus primarily on
Andy's attempts at finding true love with Ian (played by Alan Boyce), a
UCLA sophomore who approaches him outside of a Laundromat (located
beside a sex club) one night, as an S&M couple passes by, its submissive
member wearing a dog collar and leash and crawling on all fours down the

sidewalk. As they begin to walk together through the streets of Los Angeles, Andy admits that he is a bit shy, and Ian shocks him when he asks if Andy is into whips, like so many of the other people at the club. As their walk continues through a huge, deserted, fluorescent-lit parking structure, Ian pauses suddenly and asks if he can kiss Andy. Feeling a bit self-conscious, Andy takes a drag of his cigarette. Ian, not waiting for a formal response, leans in and kisses Andy tenderly on the lips, before Andy releases the puff of smoke he had inhaled. Ian then kisses Andy far more sensually before asking him out on a date, stating how physically attracted he is to him. They agree to see the Kamikaze Dildoes playing at the Hellhole on Friday night.

Following that show, Andy and Ian decide to get high together before returning to Ian's apartment, where they end up naked in bed together. Andy asks what Ian would like to do, and he is taken slightly aback at Ian's response: "Everything." Keeping in mind his personal aversion to anal intercourse, Andy asks for clarification of what Ian means by this but the young man remains vague, explaining that he plans to start by licking the tip of Andy's penis and to allow nature to take its course from there. The next day, during a conversation with Tommy, Andy reveals that he actually allowed Ian to "stuff" him, which Tommy takes as an indication that Andy is in love. That evening, however, as they continue to wander the L.A. streets trying to find something to do on a Saturday night, Andy and Ian seem to be a bit bored being together. They continue to spend time (and presumably to sleep together) over the next few days nevertheless. Then, one morning after Ian emerges from his shower to greet Andy at the nearby bathroom mirror, they hear the telephone ringing in the adjacent room and Ian rushes to answer it. Speaking in hushed tones, he tells the individual on the other end of the line that he is about to head out the door and will return the call that evening. When Andy asks who was on the phone, Ian lies by claiming it was his mother, who was calling to remind him to eat right, study hard, and that the check is in the mail.

As Andy's relationship with Ian blossoms and begins to unfold, his closest male friends are experiencing equally as emotional developments in their own lives. Tommy, for example, panics when he discovers that he has a fever and is sweating profusely, jumping to the conclusion that he is likely infected with AIDS rather than the flu, but he then engages in a very casual sexual encounter with a slightly older man in a car shortly thereafter, before being kicked out of his home by his parents when they discover that he is gay. Steven begins cheating on Deric by having an affair—and extremely hot sex—with a handsome young man who is a regular customer at the video store where he works. Deric breaks up with Steven after learning of his partner's infidelity when he watches Steven's confessional video footage while waiting for Steven in his editing room, and he ends up being bashed in an alley by a group of three golf-club-wielding thugs while walking home alone one evening, which lands him in the emergency room. In contrast, life for Andy's closest female friends, Michele and Patricia, remains entirely unchanged, with the exception that Michele begins providing continual nurturing and emotional support to Steven following his breakup with Deric, and Patricia does the same for Deric.

When Andy joins his group of queer friends at the hospital to check on Deric's condition, although he is relieved to learn that Deric will be fine, he is nevertheless quite shaken by the intensity of what has occurred. Seeking comfort himself, he heads to Ian's apartment in the middle of the night, despite the reality that Ian had stood him up earlier that evening when they were supposed to go out. It is perhaps unsurprising, therefore, that the bare-chested Ian informs Andy that he cannot come in because he is not alone. When Ian asks if it will be okay if he calls Andy the next day, Andy makes it clear that it is *not* okay. A brokenhearted Andy then rides his bicycle furiously into the night. He resurfaces a short time later, after crossing Ian's name off of his telephone's speed-dial list, where he is seen wandering through sleazy L.A. shops and grimy alleyways and going home with an anonymous stranger, whom he allows to anally penetrate him.

Given everything that has been described of the film's contents up to this point, if this were where *Totally F***ed Up* actually ends, then Araki's trademark style as an auteur director would be remarkably similar in this film as in its predecessor, *The Living End*. In both of these films, for example, Araki prominently features provocative images of non-heterosexual sexual activity and features seemingly random acts of violence (such as Deric's bashing incident, or a scene in which Andy informs Ian of a serial killer who is murdering Hollywood's hustlers, cutting off their penises, and stuffing their penises in their mouths for others to discover). In addition, he continues to defy cinematic convention with regard to content, form, (sub)genre, and linearity in this film; embraces a variety of human sexualities and sexual practices that have historically been marginalized by mainstream society (although, alas, he still does not do very much with his non-heterosexual female characters here in comparison to his non-heterosexual male characters: "It's annoying to introduce two gay women and then use them strictly for shoulders to cry on and bitchy punch lines," one critic laments [Whitty, par. 15]); favors somewhat lengthy scenes that play out in real time (most notably with Andy and Ian's walking-and-talking sequences); includes regular doses of bizarre street people and other marginal characters who populate a seemingly surrealistic Los Angeles (such as the aforementioned S&M couple featuring a dog-slave who crawls along the sidewalk, or an enraged woman standing beneath a huge billboard for Las Vegas' Excalibur hotel and casino who is screaming to absolutely nobody, or a crazed, blood-soaked woman, being chased by a hospital orderly, who crashes through the core group of central characters as they are standing outside the hospital in the aftermath of Deric's attack); and demonstrates an intentional lack of traditional commercial appeal. Where *Totally F***ed Up* differs substantially from *The Living End* and the films that come after it, however, with regard to Araki's trademark authorial style, is that, with *Totally F***ed Up*, the director takes the subject matter of his film a bit too seriously, to the extent that his treatment of it ultimately comes across as being just a bit too heavy-handed.

In the concluding sequence to *Totally F***ed Up*, seemingly out of nowhere, Andy suddenly commits suicide. Although it is clear that he is disappointed about his failed relationship with Ian, Andy nevertheless manages to bring a red rose to the recovering Deric to make him feel better about the violent incident he has experienced (as well as his recent breakup with Steven), and he does not appear to be visibly upset at all when he informs Deric that his relationship with Ian has come to an end. Nevertheless, after allowing himself to be "buttfucked" by the anonymous stranger who picks him up, Andy is shown looking a bit stressed out for a few seconds in the light of day, and he returns home in an inexplicably anxious and agitated state. There is no answer when he phones Steven, who has just stepped into the shower. He gets a busy signal when he calls both Deric and Michele, who are already engaged in a telephone conversation of their own. For no apparent reason whatsoever, Andy then walks into the kitchen of his home, where he pours himself a huge glass of whiskey, chugs some down, and adds Mop & Glo as well as a variety of additional household cleaning products to the portion that remains. After staring at the resulting concoction for a few seconds, Andy raises the glass to his lips with both hands, drinks it, and stumbles outside to his backyard, where he spits up some blood, plunges into the in-ground swimming pool, and drowns. The film concludes with Steven, Michele, Patricia, Deric, and Tommy watching video footage of Andy, in which he explains that all he has ever wanted is to be happy in life, even for one second, and to enjoy life while is he still young enough to fully appreciate it. Immediately thereafter, Steven walks over to the monitor, turns it off, and the entire screen goes black.

It is clear, from the opening seconds of *Totally F***ed Up*, that Araki intends to make a film about queer teen suicide, as the film's opening image is the text of a newspaper article titled "Suicide Rate High Among Gay Teens," which goes on to explain how 30 percent of teenagers who kill themselves are queer, and that they frequently do so after becoming despondent over their failure to succeed in life according to heterosexual expectations. The article concludes by citing the example of two teenage male lovers in Wisconsin who engaged in a double suicide after their families

decided to move apart. For viewers who may have overlooked the significance of this article to the film's narrative, Ian reiterates the boys' story to
Andy, as they walk through a gas station, by stating that the two fifteen-
year-old "secret lovers" blew each other's brains out using their fathers'
hunting rifles because they could not stand the thought of being separated,
which Andy acknowledges is sad but also very romantic. So perhaps it
should be no surprise, then, that one of the central characters in *Totally
F***ed Up* ends up committing suicide by the time the closing credits begin
to roll. This sort of heavy-handed approach to the film's overall contents,
however, is quite atypical for Araki, especially given his more open-ended
treatment of the subject matter and far more ambiguous ending of *The Living
End*, and it does not make a great deal of sense given everything else that
occurs in this film.

Examination of Araki's original screenplay for *Totally F***ed Up* reveals that the writer-director initially planned to be even *more* heavy-handed
with his treatment of this film's subject matter, as the script was originally
intended to serve, like *The Living End*, as yet another story about AIDS specifically. This reality serves to explain the inclusion of the aforementioned
scene from the final film in which a disturbing AIDS public service an-
nouncement fills the screen, as well as the one in which the highly promiscuous Tommy, suffering from a high fever and sweating profusely, fears that
he has likely contracted HIV/AIDS as a result of his sexual ways. It also
serves to explain why Andy, when encountering a young panhandler with
AIDS on an L.A. sidewalk while wandering with Ian, demonstrates compassion for the man by providing him with a dollar while Ian claims that he personally has no spare change at all to contribute.

In Araki's original screenplay, while sharing their views of safe sex,
Steven expresses hope that scientists will one day find the "magic cure" that
will eliminate the need for people to engage in it (Araki, *Totally* Screenplay
19), Deric explains that AIDS has made gay men more respectful because
they can now treat one another like human beings (rather than simply "stiff
cocks frantically trying to get off and move on to the next conquest") and
avoid "feeling the need to go to a bathhouse every Saturday night to buttfuck
some stranger" (Araki, *Totally* Screenplay 20), Tommy admits that he is
careful *most* of the time but does not want to spend his entire life worrying
about his T-cell count (Araki, *Totally* Screenplay, 21-22), and Andy expresses that he has never been tested for AIDS—and never will be (Araki,
Totally Screenplay 22). Also in Araki's original screenplay, Deric's bashers,
as they begin to assault him, refer to him as "faggot" and ask if he has AIDS
yet (Araki, *Totally* Screenplay 87).

Most notably of all in the original screenplay, however, Araki has Andy
emerging from a sterile office building, with a sign over his head reading

"Confidential Testing" (Araki, *Totally* Screenplay 97). (This appears to be the aforementioned scene that actually appears in the final film, minus the overhead sign, during which Andy is shown looking a bit stressed out for a few seconds in the light of day.) A bit later in the screenplay, Andy is shown chain-smoking and checking his watch, taking a deep breath, grabbing the telephone receiver, and punching the numbers contained on the piece of paper in his hands (Araki, *Totally* Screenplay 100). His pale face and blank expression as he hangs up the phone, coupled with the description that he is now "like someone facing a firing squad," indicate that he is either HIV positive or has developed full-blown AIDS (Araki, *Totally* Screenplay 101). This (deleted) plot development explains why he frantically begins telephoning his various friends in an anxious and agitated state, as well as why he ends up committing suicide so readily when he is unable to reach them. It appears, therefore, that Araki himself realized that he was being a bit too heavy-handed with his initially intended treatment of the subject matter of *Totally F***ed Up*, to the extent that he eliminated these various AIDS-related scenes in a conscious effort to be a bit less "preachy" and tactless in communicating the film's intended messages. In doing so, however, he actually ended up creating a narrative that does not fully add up when all is said and done, and one that appears to be even a bit *more* "preachy" and tactless with regard to the message about queer teenage suicide that it ultimately delivers as a result. (Even the casting of Alan Boyce in this film, who had previously played a high school student who commits suicide in *Permanent Record* [Marisa Silver, 1988], contributes further to this unfortunate state of affairs.) In short, Araki ends up beating the viewer over the head with the film's primary message pertaining to queer teen suicide, in an off-putting way, in much the same way that Deric is beaten over the head with golf clubs by the group of gaybashers who assault him.

Despite this glaring misstep in the film with regard to the ongoing development of Araki's authorial style, *Totally F***ed Up* nevertheless offers a unique brand of realism with regard to the cinematic exploration of the lives of contemporary (queer) teens, one that has rarely been captured on film. To increase the verisimilitude of this offering, Araki based many of the film's key plot points on real-life happenings that he had heard about. As he explains:

> One of the initial sparks was the article about the disproportionate percentage of gay teen suicides which begins the film. Another was a small news item I read about a troubled gay boy who killed himself by drinking Drano and drowning in his family's swimming pool. Then there was the lesbian acquaintance who told me about the turkey-baster insemination party she had attended. And I felt a need to respond to the unrelenting barrage of in-

stitutionalized homophobia—from the media, from ignorant politicians, from rabid cultural "watchdogs." (Araki, "Filmmaker's" 7)

Perhaps the reason that this film appears to represent a minor setback in the refinement of the director's authorial style, as compared to *The Living End*, is that Araki wrote both scripts during the same time period and *Totally F***ed Up* actually ended up being shot first; it was uncertain for a while which of the two would ultimately become his third feature (Araki, "Production" 8; Chang 50). Whatever the case, Araki's trademark style as an auteur director continued to evolve in meaningful ways in *Totally F***ed Up*, and it achieved its ideal state of development in his subsequent feature, *The Doom Generation*.

Perfecting an Authorial Style with *The Doom Generation*

The Doom Generation begins with bodies slam-dancing in a dark, rave-like environment, adjacent to the words "Welcome to hell," the letters of which have been cut out and are backlit by raging flames. A bored teenage girl, whom the viewer soon learns is Amy (played by Rose McGowan), is joined by her teenage boyfriend, Jordan (played by James Duval, the actor who played Andy in *Totally F***ed Up*), as he stops dancing and emerges from the darkness. Wanting to please the object of his affection, who clearly wants to leave, Jordan asks if Amy wants to go to "heaven." Once they are there, "heaven" is revealed to be a nearly vacant drive-in movie theater parking lot where, on this evening, the couple parks to have sex for the first time, as several other young people hang out skateboarding and drinking alcoholic beverages nearby. As their sexual encounter begins to heat up, Amy demands that Jordan put his dick in her immediately. He refuses to do so, however, because he is afraid of contracting HIV/AIDS. Amy's reassurance that they are both virgins, so that is highly unlikely to happen, falls on deaf ears. Sitting back up, Jordan comments that he feels very strange on this evening, as if something substantial is about to happen.

As their conversation continues, Amy expresses that the city of Los Angeles, in which they both live, is sucking away at her soul. Jordan responds that he feels the same way, as if he has become akin to a "gerbil smothering in Richard Gere's butthole." They begin to kiss tenderly, acknowledging that there is just no place for them in this world. Their moment of intimacy is immediately interrupted, however, as the attractive face of a young male drifter named Xavier (played by Johnathon Schaech) is forced violently against the windshield of Amy's car by a group of four males who are attacking him. The leader of this gang, who calls Xavier a "cocksucker" and informs him that his time has come to die, begins to strangle the young drifter, but Xavier successfully fights back, first delivering a powerful punch and then stabbing the man with a knife. As the other attackers back away momentarily, Xavier jumps in the back seat of Amy's car and orders her to make a fast escape. She does, but as they speed away Amy becomes increasingly concerned that Xavier is getting blood all over her vehicle's upholstery, so Jordan gives Xavier permission to use his shirt to absorb the red fluid as it pours from his leg.

With this intriguing opening sequence, Araki effectively introduces the viewer to the repressive, alienating world of these three rootless young people in the age of AIDS as well as Amy and Jordan to the bisexual drifter who will ultimately accompany them on a road trip to nowhere, in the aftermath of their (unintentionally) murdering a Quickie Mart owner and several additional individuals who disapprove of their lifestyle and intend to do them personal harm. As Amy and Jordan quickly learn, Xavier, despite being of a comparable age to them, is far more worldly and sexually experienced than they are. Shortly after they kill the Korean Quickie Mart owner who aimed a rifle at Amy and Jordan when they discovered that they did not have cash with them to pay for their desired food items (in the scene described at length at the start of chapter 1), the trio take shelter in a hotel room that is entirely red, which signifies not only the blood that they have caused to spill but also the passion among them that is percolating beneath the surface. After Xavier attempts (for the first time) to subtly seduce Jordan, while Amy takes a bath, the clueless boy fails to pick up on Xavier's intentions and proceeds to the bathroom, where he first urinates and then has sex with his girlfriend in the tub. Xavier, watching them (and focusing his gaze primarily on Jordan) through the door that is slightly ajar, masturbates the entire time and, upon shooting his load, proceeds to lick the resulting pool of ejaculate from his hand.

As the film progresses, Xavier begins to have increasingly kinky sex with Amy in order ultimately to lure her boyfriend into bed. For example, he teaches Amy to insert her finger gently into a man's anus in order to increase his sexual pleasure during intercourse; when she tries this move with Jordan, he protests, indicating that there is no way he is going to like her finger being shoved up his "shit chute," but he soon begins to enjoy the sensation. It is not long before Jordan himself assumes the role of voyeur, watching Xavier and Amy engage in a round of animalistic sex from outside a hotel window, taking out his penis and masturbating all the while. It is also not long before Xavier successfully lands Jordan in bed, at first during a sexual three-way with Amy, and then individually when she steps away from that encounter. Clearly, just as Luke "corrupts" Jon in *The Living End* and leads the young man to behave increasingly like him, Xavier has a very similar effect on Jordan, leading him to engage in more risqué forms of sexual activity and to explore the possibility of claiming a bisexual sexual orientation as his own.

As in *The Living End*, Araki once again places his young sexual adventurers on the road, playing with generic conventions and expectations by prominently featuring the theme of bisexuality in a road movie but then, on the surface at least, appearing to downplay that reality by subtitling this film, in its opening credits, as "a heterosexual movie by Gregg Araki." By freeing these characters from the confinement of their everyday locales, Araki effectively creates a utopic space within which they are able to freely explore their most intimate desires, both sexual and otherwise, in scenes that tend to border on the pornographic. Xavier appears to be the most comfortable in this sort of unstable setting, which is unsurprising given that he is a drifter whose typical relationships last three days, and sometimes only three hours. Amid his various travels he has gotten a tattoo of Jesus on his penis (so that the individuals he is fucking can say they've got Jesus inside them) and killed an annoying female parking cop (among various other individuals), and prior to those journeys he had sex with his family's dog, which he describes as having been a consenting adult. In contrast, Amy, who refers to their new traveling companion as a "life support system for a cock," initially feels a bit guilty about having wild sex outside of her relationship with Jordan but draws the line at participating in a golden shower, and Jordan takes the longest of the three to embrace new kinds of sexual experiences, not knowing that Xavier has pumped Amy for all of the intimate details about the size and shape of his cock and how he prefers to use it, but feeling reassured that Xavier, too, gets an erection when slam-dancing with other men.

Much of the violence in *The Doom Generation* is handled in a humorous way, such as when the decapitated head of the Korean Quickie Mart owner, which has flown halfway across the store to land in a tray of hotdog condiments, unexpectedly comes back to life and tries to speak, a green substance emanating from its mouth, or when Xavier hops into the back seat of Amy's car still carrying another victim's severed arm, which he eventually throws at its original possessor, hitting the man in the head with it. Although somewhat disconcerting, these violent episodes are carried out in such over-the-top ways that it is impossible for the viewer to take them very seriously. In dramatic contrast to them, however, is the extremely violent episode that composes the film's powerful concluding sequence, which certainly tests the gag reflexes of its viewers. Araki sets up the viewer to expect comedic violence throughout this offering and then, without warning, serves up startling visceral violence in its place.

During this climactic sequence, the trio discover an abandoned ware-house (which conveniently has a sheet-covered mattress on the floor) and decide to spend the night. Amy tosses a coin to determine whether she will have sex first with Xavier or Jordan on this evening. Losing the coin toss, Jordan heads outside to the car to await his turn. When Xavier eventually joins him there, the drifter once again attempts to seduce Jordan by placing their faces side by side, close enough for them to kiss, but Jordan, feeling a bit self-conscious, rises and heads back inside to have sex with Amy. As he builds toward his orgasm, Jordan is at first startled when the naked Xavier returns and climbs atop him, but the three begin to have sex together. Amy interrupts the action because she feels the urgent need to urinate; she heads outside to relieve herself, leaving the two young men in bed together, alone.

Xavier makes it clear that he is in absolutely no danger of losing his erection in Amy's absence, and he moves in once again to kiss Jordan, in the utopic setting within which they may finally consummate their growing sex-ual attraction. Just then, an unexpected development occurs: an as-yet-unseen intruder extinguishes their fire with a bucket of water. As they now sit together in total darkness, not knowing what has become of Amy, they listen as an as-yet-unidentified male voice recites a "mature" nursery rhyme that doubles as a serious threat to their well-being: "Two little faggots sittin' in a bed / One eatin' ass and the other givin' head / Dirty, perverted scum make me see red / World'll be a purer place when they're both dead." A powerful punch is landed somewhere nearby; the sound of tape being torn is heard. A strobe light begins to blink on and off, providing only brief glimpses into what is happening in the warehouse before everything goes dark again (this is the same strobe-light effect that Araki uses in *Totally F***ed Up* to heighten the emotionality of Deric's bashing at the hands of his three homophobic attackers).

As Jordan sits in a terrified, frozen position, noticing that Xavier has been knocked unconscious nearby, two neo-Nazi male thugs, sporting tube socks over their genitals and spray-painted red swastikas on their chests, grab him from behind, as their similarly attired leader dramatically unfolds an American flag on the floor. Ordering one of his fellow attackers to begin playing their favorite song, "The Star-Spangled Banner," on a boom box they have brought with them, the leader throws Amy down onto the flag and begins to rape her, while he loudly recites "The Pledge of Allegiance." Un-willing to be on the receiving end of yet another violent or aggressive act, Amy knees her attacker in the groin, infuriating him still further, which mo-tivates him to pull out a sizable porcelain figurine of the Virgin Mary and threaten to insert it inside of her. Jordan, still being held in place by the other two assailants, verbally expresses his objections to what he is witnessing; to distract Amy's rapist, Jordan makes a lewd comment about the young man's mother. The offended thug then walks over to Jordan menacingly, punches him repeatedly in his stomach, tells him that his time has come to die, and pulls out a large pair of gardening shears, which he intends to use to cut off Jordan's "puny, worthless cock." The fear in Jordan's eyes is palpable as the thug runs the shears threateningly down his torso before, as promised, he uses them to cut off Jordan's penis, which he then inserts into Xavier's mouth (in a manner akin to that mentioned in *Totally F***ed Up*, when Andy informs Ian of the actions of the serial killer who is preying on Hollywood hustlers). This extreme, entirely unexpected bloodbath continues as Amy uses the same pair of gardening shears to kill Jordan's attacker, and Xavier assists her in killing the other two thugs.

This powerful concluding sequence typically leaves first-time viewers of *The Doom Generation* in a mild state of shock, many of whom are unable to make sense of its significance and are turned off to the film in its entirety as a result, if they did not already feel that way prior to its occurrence (Hart, "Cinematic" 53-69). Numerous critics share this reaction to the film. For example, the group of reviewers known collectively as the Mutant Reviewers from Hell, who are typically quite open-minded to unique and unconventional approaches to filmmaking, capture the negative reactions of their various counterparts in their series of reviews of this film. Mutant Reviewer Clare writes, "So is *The Doom Generation* supposed to be a cheeky comedy that just fails miserably or is it supposed to be a serious look at the tangled web we weave when at first we practice to explore our sexuality while simultaneously killing bystanders indiscriminately? My quick and dirty answer? Who cares?" (par. 1). Mutant Reviewer Justin states:

> Sometimes you see such an awful movie that you need to tell people about it to purge the memory from your system. Sometimes you see such a horribly awful movie that you would like to find the makers of the film and do mean things to their pets. Sometimes you see such a piece of crap that you yank off your clothes, cover yourself with ashes, and go out onto the street with a sandwich board proclaiming that the end of the world is coming, because movies this horribly putridly awful are being made. (par. 1)

Mutant Reviewer Kyle expresses, "This film hurts you. It ruined my day when I rented it, just because it did succeed in catching the events in depressing lives of people scraped from the bottom of the scum barrel. Gross people doing gross things, conceived by people who should never have made a film in the first place" (par. 2).

Other critics have referred to *The Doom Generation* as "a difficult film to consume, even by those who proclaim themselves to be the kings and/or queens of ultra-bizarre underground cinema . . . and [those] who would like nothing more than to burn every single copy they can get their self-important little hands on" (Film Fiend, par. 2), "hands-down one of the most horrid examples of filmmaking I've seen in ages" (Null, par. 1), and "the kind of movie where the filmmaker hopes to shock you with sickening carnage and violent amorality" (Ebert, par. 1). When reviewing this film in the *Chicago Sun-Times* shortly after its initial release, critic Roger Ebert refused to award it any stars whatsoever.

What is likely evident from those reviews, and so many others like them, is that Araki's impeccable application of his trademark in-your-face authorial style in *The Doom Generation*, which he has perfected with this offering, is off-putting to many viewers and critics. At the same time, that is what makes his directorial style so radical and potentially subversive. Viewers and critics who take the time to reflect carefully on the contents of this film (and, in particular, its highly disturbing concluding sequence) and refuse to readily dismiss it as a leading example of cinematic trash will discover an intelligent, carefully crafted, and fulfilling cinematic offering that communicates an incredibly powerful message about the highly "repressive nature of hegemonic ideology in the United States in relation to bisexual men and other non-heterosexual individuals" (Hart, "Cinematic" 55). Film critics Matthew Severson and Robin Wood are among the comparatively much smaller number of individuals who apparently achieve such a level of insight as they have written, respectively, that with this film "Araki has made a more radical personal and political film than the bombastic [Oliver] Stone, [the director of *Natural Born Killers* (1994)], could have managed in his wettest of wet dreams, and he has captured the cultural apathy and violent dissolution of the present in a manner unseen since *A Clockwork Orange* [Stanley Kubrick, 1971]" (Severson, par. 1) and that "*The Doom Generation* is a powerfully political film . . . [with] the film's culmination represent[ing] one of the most radical political statements in American cinema" (Wood 339).

Viewers who like to sit through a film's closing credits learn that the characters' last names in *The Doom Generation* are (Xavier) Red, (Jordan) White, and (Amy) Blue. This reality, coupled with the startling use of the American flag, "The Star-Spangled Banner," and "The Pledge of Allegiance," strongly suggests that Araki's film is consciously intended to serve as a condemning commentary on the repressive nature of U.S. ideology in relation to sexual "outlaws." Although a surface-level reading of the film's narrative suggests that diversity in the form of non-heterosexual sexual orientations and/or non-monogamous (threesome) relationships is what endangers the well-being of individuals in U.S. society, careful consideration of the work's latent content indicates that it is actually social and religious conservatism that most greatly endangers such well-being, and that there are people in this world, such as the trio's attackers at the film's end who are acting on the behalf of such conservatism, who are the real "outlaws" that must be feared. As film scholar James Moran has noted:

> Although fierce in its implicit attack upon a conservative American society condoning only heterosexuality at the violent expense of all other unconventional unions (thus explaining the irreverent irony of *Doom*'s subtitle), the film's politics function primarily as subtext, averting an explicit confrontation of the causes of institutionalized homophobia by hyperdramatizing its hideous effects in an over-the-top display of savagery. (23)

By vividly and unconventionally revealing the progress that remains to be made with regard to the true acceptance of non-heterosexual identities, *The Doom Generation* simultaneously offers hope for a very different sort of future in which alienation, discrimination, and condemnation will become phenomena of the past as Amy and Xavier, in the aftermath of Jordan's murder, drive off toward a destination yet unknown.

Concluding Observations

Without question, *The Doom Generation*, which Araki intended to be "as far out and surreal as possible, like a bad drug trip" ("Interview," par. 11), maximizes the effectiveness of the director's trademark post-punk style, as developed in his earlier films and perfected in this offering. This style serves simultaneously as the "essence" of Araki's filmmaking as well as the source of its radical/subversive potential. As summarized a bit earlier in this chapter, during the analysis of *Totally F***ed Up*, the hallmarks of Araki's authorial style include provocative images of non-heterosexual sexual activity and seemingly random acts of violence; defiance of cinematic convention with regard to content, form, (sub)genre, and linearity; the foregrounding of a variety of human sexualities and sexual practices that have historically been marginalized by mainstream society; lengthy scenes that play out in real time to heighten their emotionality; the regular inclusion of bizarre street people and other marginal characters who populate a seemingly surrealistic Los Angeles; an intentional lack of traditional commercial appeal; and the unabashed refusal to take the films and their subject matter entirely seriously. This latter attribute serves to explain why, despite the severity of its concluding sequence and the sobering message about U.S. society that it is attempting to communicate, *The Doom Generation* is peppered with repeated references to the number "666" (which is the total of virtually everything the trio buys, the street address of one of their hotels, and Amy's cumulative SAT score), apocalyptic signs everywhere (which read "The rapture is coming," "Prepare for the apocalypse," "Pray for your lost soul," and the like), random nursery rhymes (including "Row, Row, Row Your Boat" and "Itsy Bitsy Spider"), and playful cameo appearances (by numerous cultural icons including Amanda Bearse, Margaret Cho, Perry Farrell, Heidi Fleiss, Christopher Knight, and Parker Posey).

Naturally, Araki's authorial style did not evolve in a creative vacuum. Although it is not always readily evident when viewing his films, he is quite familiar with the works and careers of auteur directors from the early years of cinema to the present, and he has repeatedly identified Jean-Luc Godard of the French New Wave in particular as one of the greatest influences on his own filmmaking style. Araki has indicated that he intentionally patterned *Totally F***ed Up* after Godard's *Masculine-Feminine* (1966) in order to pay tribute to that masterpiece by making his own kind of *Masculine-Feminine* about gay teens—in fact, he cut his original screenplay from twenty-one "random celluloid fragments" down to only fifteen, at least in part, because *Masculine-Feminine* contains only fifteen segments—and there are clear parallels in *The Doom Generation* to Godard's demented road-movie approach in *Weekend* (1967) (Severson, par. 21-22; Hart, "Auteur" 32-33). In addition, instances of Godard-inspired lighting, editing, jumpcuts, intertitles, direct address, free-associative narrative, nonlinearity, and related attributes abound in Araki's various films. In recognition of Godard's substantial influence on Araki's filmmaking style, James Moran has emphasized:

> Godard, in fact, is perhaps the figure most representative of Araki's conception of the independent who can work within the institution of cinema in order to change it. The disjointed techniques of Godard's early work, in particular *Breathless* [1959] and *Weekend*, are evident in Araki's films, as is the interminable banality of faceless locales pocked with strip malls, fast-food joints, and deserted parking lots, disturbed only by the aimless wanderings of anomic urban neurotics. Together, the protagonists' names in *The Living End* are Jon Luke, and if that weren't enough, a "Made in U.S.A." poster adorns Jon's bedroom. While these Godardian touches are at times more precocious than provocative, Araki's narrative experiments do find fruition in *Totally F***ed Up*, a diary-like compendium that records the everyday hopes and frustrations of a close circle of gay and lesbian teens, as well as their somewhat jaundiced views of the culture on whose margins they find themselves surviving. (20)

Araki's filmmaking style has been described by one critic as "marrying Godardian cinematic style with industrial music" ("Designed, par. 2), and that appears to be an accurate assessment of key components of the director's post-punk style. Like punk musical offerings in their heyday, with which he is quite familiar as a result of his enthusiastic participation in the West Coast punk-rock scene during the late 1970s and early 1980s, Araki's films are readily identifiable by their rawness, aggressive energy, nihilistic themes, disconcerting tone, and potent spirit of anarchy and disorder, which is intended to challenge influential hegemonic conceptions pertaining to ideology and social order as well as repressive social expectations and gender/sex roles. They regularly subvert genre conventions and expectations in order to subvert their established meanings and significance, and they do so in order to create groundbreaking representations of non-heterosexual individuals and subcultures. They are not particularly concerned with political correctness, commercial viability, or conventional mainstream appeal.

As Araki, a self-described "black sheep, punk-rock, artistic kid" (Asch, par. 10), himself has stated, "The more radical and subversive elements of my movies are kind of like the punk rock music of the late '70s and early '80s, [when] punk was viewed as being very far out of the mainstream" (Asch, par. 16). He elaborates: "My whole thing, all my life, was 'march to your own drummer'. . . . I was always very much an individual, and that's why I was so deeply influenced by punk-rock culture and post-punk culture, because there's that whole DIY thing, the go-against-the-corporate-mentality sort of approach. I think that's probably my major influence in terms of my sensibility" (D. Smith, par. 21).

The radical/subversive potential of Araki's post-punk filmmaking approach is perhaps best summed up by James Duval, who played both Andy in *Totally F***ed Up* and Jordan in *The Doom Generation*, with regard to the latter film: "[I]t's mixed with a lot of socially conscious issues and brings them into light. It really challenges the way people think and feel and see certain situations. It's interesting because I think *Doom* is full of social issues but you don't really see 'em; they're beneath the surface and subtle" ("Interview," par. 9). That reality stands in stark contrast to Araki's treatment of his subject matter in *Totally F***ed Up*, which ends up being far less effective and intriguing because it is so heavy-handed.

Armed with the distinctive, in-your-face, post-punk authorial style that he continued to refine in *Totally F***ed Up* and perfected in *The Doom Generation*, Araki appeared poised to create his most effective teen-apocalypse feature yet as he began work in earnest on *Nowhere*, the final film in his planned trilogy. It would be two years before his fans would learn whether his next creation would live up to that potential.

Chapter 4
Losing Focus with *Nowhere* and *Splendor*

Following the release of *The Doom Generation*, loyal Gregg Araki fans likely believed, beyond the shadow of a doubt, that they knew exactly what they could expect from any forthcoming Araki film: provocative images of non-heterosexual sexual activity and acts of visceral violence; defiance of cinematic convention; unapologetic foregrounding of a range of human sexualities and sexual practices that have historically been marginalized by mainstream society; lengthy scenes that play out in real time to heighten their emotionality; regular inclusion of bizarre, marginal characters who populate a seemingly surrealistic Los Angeles; intentional lack of traditional commercial appeal; and intentional refusal to take the films and their subject matter too seriously—all of which are utilized skillfully to make a powerful statement about non-heterosexuality and non-heterosexual individuals living in the age of AIDS. Unfortunately, those who held such a belief were also very likely disappointed by the overall contents of the director's next two films: *Nowhere* (1997), the final offering of Araki's teen-apocalypse trilogy, and *Splendor* (1999), a romantic comedy about three creative, heterosexual young adults (one woman and two men) who enter into an unconventional familial and romantic relationship.

Without question, *The Doom Generation* was a transitional work for Araki, primarily because it was his first film made with a sizable budget (of approximately one million dollars, from French investors), which enabled him to work with a professional cinematographer, a production designer, and SAG actors for the first time as well as to give up many of his guerilla-filmmaking ways (Chang 47; Cooper 22; Moran 20; Severson, par. 3). It was also a film that was off-putting to critics, many of whom walked out of its initial press screening, where the work played to an almost entirely silent audience (Severson, par. 5). At the time, film scholar James Moran argued

51

that such realities would not result in a newfound aesthetic for Araki, but rather that they would simply enable the auteur director to realize his post-punk "sensibility at a greater level of ambition" (Moran 20). Araki himself echoed such sentiments, in 1995, when he stated, "Even if I were to make a fifty-million-dollar movie, because my personality is very strong, it would be a high-budget Gregg Araki film. I'm not too concerned about being sucked up into making faceless movies" (qtd. in Moran 20). Araki further emphasized that his films would continue to differ substantially from main-stream Hollywood offerings, because "any 'independent' film that reinforces and buys into the values of the mainstream is an opportunity wasted" (qtd. in Moran 20).

Despite such claims and assurances, however, the contents of Araki's next two films differed substantially from those that came before them. Per-haps most notably, although *Nowhere* contains many elements of Araki's trademark post-punk authorial style and *Splendor* far fewer of those ele-ments, both of these films nevertheless possess a dramatically reduced radi-cal/subversive potential as compared with Araki's preceding films and their unapologetic representations of non-heterosexuality. These works represent the "straightest" creations of Araki's career up to the times of their release, even though they retain faint glimpses of the director's established queer sensibility, and it is evident that their character types and on-screen actions became more tame as investor expectations for their financial returns con-tinued to grow.

Taming (Teen) Queerness with *Nowhere*

With *Nowhere*, as he had done with both *Totally F***ed Up* and *The Doom Generation*, Araki set out to create a romantic film, with a "weird surrealis-tic tinge, buffered with real-world reality and serious spasms of ultra-violence," that focuses primarily on generational confusion and the possibil-ity of love and is experienced like a crazy roller-coaster ride ("Gregg's," par. 6, 16). This time around, however, he intentionally wrote the script in the form of a television pilot: "*Nowhere*, my next movie, is going to be my ver-sion of *Beverly Hills 90210*, that whole idea of the interrelationships be-tween beautiful L.A. youth. It's a mainstream movie with mainstream con-tent, but totally tweaked and totally twisted and totally me," Araki explained in a 1994 interview (Chang 53). The fact that Araki admitted to intentionally creating a "mainstream movie with mainstream content" must not be over-looked, as this offering represents a substantial turning point in his film-making career that reached its apex with *Splendor* just a few years later. Whereas Araki's preceding films appeared intentionally to attract controversy as a result of their unapologetic, in-your-face representations of non-heterosexual sexual orientations and forms of sexual expression, *Nowhere* and *Splendor* instead appeared to endeavor intentionally to downplay the risks of attracting such controversy while at the same time remaining just a bit beyond the mainstream.

Nowhere provides a (presumably typical) day-in-the-life glimpse into the everyday realities of a large group of racially and ethnically diverse L.A. adolescents and the feelings of alienation and insecurity that they regularly experience. As he did in both of the preceding offerings of Araki's teen-apocalypse trilogy, actor James Duval once again stars in the central role of this film as Dark, an attractive eighteen year old who believes that he and the other members of his generation were born to witness the end of the world and hopes, as a result, to find his one true love before the apocalypse occurs. Although he is romantically and sexually involved with Mel (played by Rachel True), she nevertheless has a purple-haired girlfriend on the side, named Lucifer (played by Kathleen Robertson), and believes in sleeping around with numerous others, of both sexes, while she is still young and attractive enough to do so. From the film's opening scene, as Dark masturbates in the shower while thinking about being alone with another bare-chested guy in a locker room, it becomes evident that he is experiencing bisexual urges of his own for Montgomery (played by Nathan Bexton), with whom he ends up in bed during the film's concluding scene.

Promoted by Fine Line Features, its distributor, as being "like a *Beverly Hills 90210* episode on acid" ("About," par. 2), *Nowhere* contains "enough characters to fill two Robert Altman movies" (Satuloff 92)—a total of nineteen central characters and approximately two dozen peripheral ones—as well as a fractured, web-like narrative that is not especially viewer-friendly. Dark's best friend, Cowboy (played by Guillermo Diaz), is experiencing difficulties with his boyfriend and fellow band member Bart (played by Jeremy Jordan), who, immersed in a self-destructive downward spiral, is becoming increasingly addicted to the substances sold to him by Handjob (played by Alan Boyce), a local drug dealer, as well as to his S&M-tinged sexual interactions with Kriss and Kozy (played by Chiara Mastroianni and Debi Mazar, respectively), the dominatrix duo who spend all of their time by the dealer's side. Montgomery requests some tutoring assistance from the brainy, brace-faced Dingbat (played by Christina Applegate), who has a major crush on Ducky (played by Scott Caan), who only has eyes for Alyssa (played by Jordan Ladd), who is sleeping with the well-endowed biker Elvis (played by Thyme Lewis). Ducky's sister, Egg (played by Sarah Lassez), is spending the day with The Teen Idol (played by Jaason Simmons) from *Baywatch*, who walked in on her while she was urinating in a coffeehouse bathroom that morning. Rounding out the film's main characters are Alyssa's twin brother, Shad (played by Ryan Phillippe), who spends all of his time engaging in kinky sex acts with his girlfriend, Lilith (played by Heather Graham)—such as inserting chocolate into her vagina and then eating out the melted remains—and Mel's younger brother, Zero (played by Joshua Gibran Mayweather), who is in puppy love with Zoe (played by Mena Suvari). *Nowhere* also features cameo appearances by Beverly D'Angelo, Shannen Doherty, Christopher Knight, David Leisure, Traci Lords, Rose McGowan, Eve Plumb, Charlotte Rae, John Ritter, and Lauren Tewes, among others, which Araki scatters throughout the film in order to reinforce its cumulative hallucinogenic quality ("About," par. 12).

Because Dark is convinced that he will die soon, he takes his video camera with him everywhere, in order to document his impending doom. While he awaits the end of the world, he and Lucifer squabble incessantly, like little children, as a result of their ongoing competition for Mel's affection (e.g., Lucifer: "Lick my box, Rover." Dark, in response: "Clean the maggots out of it first, you stinky oyster"), and he and his friends enjoy hanging out and taking hallucinogenic drugs together, such as when they play a game of "kick the can" while on Ecstasy. Occasional acts of visceral violence emerge suddenly in the film, without any foreshadowing whatsoever, such as when Egg's seeming storybook romance with The Teen Idol comes to an abrupt end when he violently rapes her after having convinced her that she is truly someone very special and getting her drunk, or when Elvis gleefully (and dementedly) beats Handjob to death with a Campbell's Tomato Soup can (an apparent homage to Andy Warhol) at a party because the dealer recently sold him some bad drugs. In addition to these unexpected plot developments, Egg suddenly commits suicide when she returns home, with dried blood covering her face, following her abuse at the hands of The Teen Idol, and Bart does the same after he returns home, feeling a bit disillusioned and alone, following a kinky sexual encounter during which Kriss and Kozy tear out both of his nipple rings, one using her teeth and the other using a pair of pliers.

Perhaps the most unexpected developments of all in the film, however, involve the green-and-yellow, Godzilla-like space alien that is roaming Los Angeles which only Dark apparently sees. He first glimpses the alien while he is waiting at a bus stop, smoking a cigarette and listening to the sex-themed conversation of three ostentatiously dressed valley girls. As he fumbles (unsuccessfully) with his video camera to capture an image of this alien being, Dark is startled to witness the creature pulling out a laser gun and vaporizing the three girls, who vanish instantly, along with the alien. That evening, during the kick-the-can-on-Ecstasy game, Dark suspects that Montgomery has also been vaporized by the alien when he finds Montgomery's crucifix necklace on the floor in a seemingly otherwise empty locker room and then, moments later, is saluted by the alien before it once again disappears. Finally, during the big party being hosted by Jujyfruit (played by Gibby Haynes) at the night's end, Dark glimpses the space alien for the final time, as it drinks a beer in the kitchen. Surprisingly, Dark mentions his various encounters with the space alien only to Handjob—casually mentioning that, in the past eighteen hours, he has witnessed four people being abducted by a space alien, a friend attempting to drown himself (in reference to Ducky's extreme reaction to the news of his sister's suicide), and nearly four hundred dollars leaving his wallet to pay for compact discs, with Handjob's response asking only about what sorts of CDs he purchased—just prior to the drug dealer being murdered by Elvis.

Alone in his bedroom at the end of the long day, during which it has become clear that Mel does not really care about him and is certainly not interested in a monogamous relationship, Dark remarks in his video-diary entry that all he wants out of life is one person who will hold him tight and reassure him that everything is going to be alright. Moments after he turns off the video camera, strips off his clothes, and switches off his bedroom light, he suddenly hears a faint tapping. Rising, he discovers the naked Montgomery, who removes a suction cup from his own forehead, at his window. After inviting him in and lending him a pair of his (dirty) underwear, Dark listens intently as Montgomery explains that he was kidnapped by space aliens, who experimented on him and talked of their intentions to take over the Earth before he was able to escape. Noting that he feels tired and a bit strange, as if catching a cold, Montgomery asks if he can rest awhile in Dark's bed. Lying down, he invites Dark to join him; Dark readily complies. Lying face-to-face with Dark, Montgomery acknowledges Dark's recent romantic relationship with Mel and then, gazing directly into Dark's eyes, emphasizes that he is not gay while simultaneously revealing his attraction toward his newfound friend. It is evident that the attraction is mutual. Montgomery proceeds to explain that he likes Dark a great deal, and that he thinks about him when they are apart; Dark responds that he feels the same way about Montgomery. When Montgomery adds that he has been searching his entire life for the one person he can love who simultaneously loves him for who he is, Dark is clearly smitten, as he leans in and kisses Montgomery on the forehead. Montgomery requests permission to spend the night, because he very much wants to sleep next to Dark. Dark grants his request based on one condition, to which Montgomery assents: that Montgomery will never, ever leave him. With their noses practically touching and their lips poised for a kiss, Dark delicately caresses Montgomery's cheek, and they close their eyes in preparation for a good night's sleep. Without question, this is the most touching scene in the film, and it is the only one that is developed in adequate depth, with Araki allowing it, in his expected trademark fashion, to play out in real time in order to emphasize its significance and heighten its emotionality. In fact, as Gavin Smith noted in *Film Comment*, this "final scene, in which [the] two boys profess their love for each other, manages to be the most heartfelt and tender moment in [Araki's] oeuvre . . ." ("Sundance 97" 55).

Unfortunately, however, this concluding scene, like so many others in the film, takes an immediate, entirely unexpected turn for the worse. Smith's comment, in its entirety, actually reads: "The final scene, in which [the] two boys profess their love for each other, manages to be the most heartfelt and tender moment in [Araki's] oeuvre—and, in its outrageous payoff, the most disillusioned" ("Sundance 97" 55). As the scene continues, Montgomery begins to cough lightly; he soon begins to cough far more violently and incessantly, as though he is in danger of gagging or choking. Dark, visibly concerned, attempts to comfort him, but to no avail—as Montgomery's entire body convulses, the boy explodes, showering Dark and the surrounding room with blood. Where an attractive male body once lay, Dark now discovers a huge cockroach-like space alien who announces "I'm outta here" and climbs out the window. A close-up of Dark's blood-covered face fills the screen as it fades to black, and the closing credits begin to roll.

On its surface, *Nowhere* is certainly a Gregg Araki film containing key elements of the director's post-punk filmmaking style—for example, it features two characters who engage in bisexual romantic and sexual relationships as well as random acts of visceral violence, defies mainstream approaches to teen films, and contains several scenes foregrounding S&M activity (including those with the dominatrix duo Kriss and Kozy as well as one in which Elvis commands Alyssa to tie him up and spank him as hard as possible) and a few foregrounding transvestitism. From start to finish, it also certainly embraces an intentional lack of traditional commercial appeal and refuses to take itself and its subject matter too seriously. A primary shortcoming of the film, however, is that it refuses to take itself and its subject matter seriously *at all*, as a result of transforming the director's trademark bizarre, marginal characters who populate a seemingly surrealistic Los Angeles from interesting backdrop to comparatively uninteresting primary focus. With so many (superficial) characters to follow and the narrative jumping continually, and quite rapidly, from one character to the next, the viewer ends up caring about none of these young people at all (with the possible exception of Dark, yet far less so here than for the characters Duval played in both *Totally F***ed Up* and *The Doom Generation*), a reality that results from the film's virtual abandonment (with the exception of its concluding scene, which ultimately goes awry) of Araki's penchant for including lengthy scenes that play out in real time to heighten their emotionality. Another glaring shortcoming of this film is that, as a result of these various factors and unlike the director's preceding works, it fails to make any sort of compelling statement about non-heterosexuality and/or non-heterosexual individuals living in the age of AIDS that Araki's fans had come to expect. When Montgomery's body explodes at the film's end, Araki ends up making only a very superficial, tongue-in-cheek, and ultimately unfulfilling statement about "alien-ation" in relation to contemporary teens. Perhaps that is all that can be expected of a film that endeavors intentionally, in both its storyline and visual style, to emulate a hallucinogenic drug trip; however, there is no denying that the work's extreme emphasis on style over substance leaves a tremendous amount to be desired by its viewer.

About this film, Araki has stated:

> I wanted to portray the world from a messed-up eighteen year old's perspective, a world within which anything can happen. When you're that age, everything is life or death, everything is hyper-accentuated. The film attempts to capture those extreme highs and lows. . . . It's about what it really feels like to be confused, to be in love, to watch your girlfriend leave the party with some other guy. ("About," par. 5, 14)

In those (somewhat simplistic) regards, *Nowhere* certainly accomplishes what its writer-director set out to do. The film's representation of teen life is entirely "messed up," and it is one that repeatedly vacillates from one extreme to the next, creating a world in which practically anything at all—including an alien invasion—can occur without warning. The problem is that, when all is said and done, the film ends up feeling inauthentic—it is clear that Araki has included all of the key components of his trademark post-punk filmmaking style here, as if he were checking them off of a comprehensive list, but the expected radical/subversive payoff fails to materialize. Critic Bob Satuloff has characterized *Nowhere* as being "like a crazy quilt into which anything can be sewn" (92); in addition, Araki himself has admitted that, with the exception of the James Duval character, *Nowhere* "really is just this bunch of crazy shit going on, with no emotional center" (Hundley, par. 12). As a result, the film ends up representing a very different—and ultimately quite disappointing—sort of creation from this formerly intriguing and quite groundbreaking director.

Following the release of *Nowhere*, numerous critics noted that it is a very different sort of Gregg Araki movie. For example, reviewing the film for *Variety*, Emanuel Levy wrote, "Though not his best, Araki's sixth feature is without a doubt his most accessible . . . and superficially entertaining movie to date" and that, as a result, the film should end up attracting a larger audience than the director's preceding offerings ("Nowhere" 66). In the same review, Levy also pointed out that "thematically, [this] film has nothing new to offer" ("Nowhere" 66). Reviewing the film for *Artforum*, Dennis

Cooper stated that Araki's career "takes a sharp turn" with *Nowhere,* a "bratty and hyperactive" offering that is filled with "phantasmagoric shallowness" as well as a "virtually interchangeable" cast of characters that "you're not supposed to give a toss about—just pick out a cutie, track him or her through the labyrinth plot, and hope he or she eventually gets naked" (22). With regard to the film's ultimate (and quite minimal) impact on the viewer, Cooper adds, "When *Nowhere* is over, it's so over that you half-wonder if Araki has invented a way to induce amnesia aesthetically" (22). Similarly, the reviewer for Film.com characterized the work as "a lighter, quicker movie than the first two-thirds of the triad [that] feels much slighter than its predecessors" and noted that, because "Araki has made the film in emulation of those hormonal hothouse TV dramas *Beverly Hills 90210* and *Melrose Place,* it veers closer to parody than the unsettling horror-slasher-comedy of *The Doom Generation*" (par. 1, 2). Reviewing the film for *Entertainment Weekly,* Lisa Schwarzbaum noted that, along with its superficial storyline, *Nowhere* features a "visual and aural overload that ultimately tires rather than conveys a feeling of f***ed up-ness" (46). Most directly of all, reviewer Jason Katzman emphasized that *Nowhere* is the type of film "jeered at not only just by critics, but also by drunken teenagers, prison inmates, and medicated zoo animals" (qtd. in Hershenson, par. 9).

During one of his heartfelt discussions with Mel, Dark states that he feels old-fashioned, as if he is from another planet, because he feels like he is only half a person without her. In another, Dark expresses to Mel that he wishes he could leave this entire planet behind in order to find true love. Such sentiments of isolation and alienation potentially lend themselves quite effectively to the creation of a science fiction narrative in which aliens from another planet begin to roam the Earth and perform experiments on humans whom they abduct, especially because science fiction works have historically devoted themselves to exploring as-yet-unknown worlds and social conditions that lie beyond known boundaries and emphasize potentially threatening deviations from the mainstream status quo (Lopez 267; Parish and Pitts vii; Shapiro 111). Accordingly, otherness in various forms is an essential component of science fiction narratives. Sometimes, such otherness results from viewer comparisons between present-day, real-world conditions and those provided in the science fiction work itself, with the aim of determining what one day might be experienced if current practices or deleterious trends are allowed to continue unabated (Hart, *AIDS* 17-18). At other times, a far more straightforward and readily identifiable incarnation of such otherness assumes the form of "the other," whether this be a physical being (e.g., alien, monster, threatening life form, etc.) or some social phenomenon (e.g., a disease, some condition that endangers human life, etc.) that deviates substantially from the mainstream status quo (Hart, *AIDS* 19). As a result, especially for a director such as Araki who is known for engaging effectively in genre modification and defiance of cinematic convention, the potentialities of incorporating elements of science fiction offerings in a teen film, with the aim of creating a particularly compelling statement about alienation and social otherness in relation to contemporary teens, cannot be overstated. Unfortunately, Araki did not adequately avail himself of these potentialities when writing and directing *Nowhere*. Instead, his incorporation of the Godzilla-like space alien in this film serves primarily to make the daily world of its far-too-numerous teen characters seem just a bit more strange and surreal and to hint at the (presumably forthcoming) apocalypse, rather than to make any sort of more complex, more intelligent statement about otherness in relation to contemporary young people. In the end, and as a result, *Nowhere* leaves many viewers desiring their money back, or at least the eighty minutes of their lives that they have devoted to the viewing experience. Even the significance of the film's title is neither particularly fulfilling nor deep: As Dark explains during the opening seconds, "L.A. is, like, nowhere—everybody who lives here is lost."

In his review of the film, Emanuel Levy concluded, "*Nowhere* is the kind of expressionistic movie that Araki had to make, though now that it's out of his system, perhaps he can move on to newer subjects—and more resonant films" ("Nowhere" 66). A similar sentiment was expressed by critic Lawrie Zion, who noted that, in this final installment of his teen-apocalypse trilogy, Araki "wallowed in pretension that . . . lacked dramatic focus" and "continued to trade on shock value, but with diminishing artistic returns" ("Truth" F14). Accordingly, in the months following *Nowhere*'s release, the director's remaining devoted fans waited with bated breath to see if Araki would redeem himself, and get his filmmaking career back on (its original) track, with the release of his next feature film.

Going Mainstream with *Splendor*

Araki had initially announced that his next film following *Nowhere* would be *The Separation of the Earth from its Axis*, the story of a gay male teen who ends up falling in love with a single father ("Personnel" 11; *Totally* Screenplay). However, by the time *Nowhere* was released, the assumedly gay director had apparently (and quite unexpectedly) become romantically involved with Kathleen Robertson, who played Lucifer in the concluding offering of his teen-apocalypse trilogy (which he dedicated to her in the closing credits with the words "I love you, honey 4ever.xxx") and who starred in what ultimately became his seventh feature instead of *The Separation of the Earth from its Axis*, the romantic comedy *Splendor* (which he also dedicated to Robertson in the closing credits: "For my baby, my one and only"). Araki's romantic relationship with a woman certainly "set tongues wagging" (Brodie 11), especially after he walked all around the Sundance Film Festival with Robertson on his arm (Hays, "Make," par. 7). It also ended up further alienating several of his earliest fans while simultaneously leading his filmmaking style and creative choices in new, far less controversial, and increasingly heterosexual directions.

Take, for example, the following scene from *Splendor*, written and directed by Araki, which is actually one of the film's most erotic. In an L.A. apartment, Veronica (played by Robertson), a heterosexual aspiring actress, invites the two men she has been dating simultaneously for several months to dinner and, after plying each with numerous drinks, initiates a game of Truth or Dare. She asks the first guy, the brooding novelist and music critic Abel (played by Johnathon Schaech), if he has ever had sex with a guy; he replies that he has not. She asks the second guy, the punk-rock drummer with perfect abs Zed (played by Matt Keeslar), the same question; "Define sex," he replies. Next, she dares Abel to remove his shirt and Zed to remove his pants. As the game progresses, the woman dares Abel to kiss Zed. He instantly refuses. Veronica expresses her disappointment, cautioning that Abel's refusal is turning her off and adding that a kiss between the two men would be incredibly hot. Reluctantly, Abel plants a quick peck on Zed's cheek. "No, you have to do it on the lips," Veronica protests, once again revealing her disappointment. Minutes later, after she has stripped naked and danced around the room on a dare, Veronica dares Zed to kiss Abel "full on." An initially tight-lipped, entirely tongue-less and passion-free kiss, lasting fewer then ten seconds, results.

If the above scene had appeared in *The Living End*, *Totally F***ed Up*, or *The Doom Generation*, the resulting kiss between these two attractive young men would have been much hotter, and they likely would have been fondling each other's package before progressing to have sex with each other, as well as with Veronica. In *Splendor*, however, that is where the scene draws to an abrupt close. The following day, during a conversation with her lesbian best friend, Mike (played by Kelly Macdonald), Veronica reveals that the three did indeed end up in bed together the previous evening; however, Veronica emphasizes that, to the best of her knowledge, nothing at all happened sexually between the two guys. Such elusive treatment of such a sexually charged situation is extremely atypical for Araki, who set out with this film to make a relatively wholesome romantic comedy focusing on a threesome relationship between a heterosexual woman and two heterosexual—not even *bisexual*—men. The main idea behind the storyline is that, when Veronica finds herself unable to choose between the two men—both of whom she met at the same Halloween party; one of whom offers intellectual stimulation and the other who provides animalistic sexuality—she decides to keep them both.

As the film continues, both men end up moving into Veronica's apartment after Zed is thrown out by his roommates for not paying the rent and Abel becomes jealous when Veronica takes him in. By summer, the three young people are, in Veronica's words, "living in sin together" as "one happy, kooky family," as if "the rules everybody else [lives] by didn't apply to [them]." Abel articulates that he doesn't care if others end up regarding them as deviant freaks because they sleep in the same bed and have sex together on a regular basis. Their biggest problem, in fact, appears to be that the guys frequently leave the toilet seat up. Such tranquility disappears quickly, however, after Veronica becomes pregnant and begins dating Ernest (played by Eric Mabius), a successful television producer and new suitor who, unlike her own parents, will be able to provide her unborn child with an affluent and stable home environment. Abel and Zed are devastated when Veronica moves out to stay with Mike for a while, in order to weigh her options and pursue her emergent romantic relationship with Ernest, which blossoms more fully during a vacation getaway to Maui. When they learn, at the last minute, that Veronica is planning to marry Ernest on New Year's Eve, however, they snap out of their depressed, inebriated states and stop the wedding, in a sequence that is clearly an homage to the interrupted wedding sequence in *The Graduate* (Mike Nichols, 1967). Thereafter, Veronica ultimately gives birth to twin girls, and she emphasizes, in response to the guys' repeated inquiries, that the daughters are neither Abel's nor Zed's. Instead, she says, "They're ours."

In reviewing the film for *Variety*, Emanuel Levy referred to *Splendor* as an "upbeat, visually stunning but inconsequential picture which holds limited commercial appeal in today's market" and noted that, "having lost his core gay audience with his teen-apocalypse trilogy (*Totally F***ed Up*, *The Doom Generation*, and *Nowhere*), all of which failed commercially, Araki [was] forced to return to the creative well and come up with a different kind of film" (62). The end result? As critic Jan Stuart explained in *The Advocate*, "Lube your gag reflex, dudes, but he's gone and made a screwball comedy. I know, I know, but give him some slack, people. Even totally rad directors get old" (63). Succinctly summarizing the film's storyline, Stuart continues:

> You *Nowhere* fans will recognize Kathleen Robertson (Araki's real-life girlfriend) looking very Melanie Griffith in blonde hair as Veronica, this ex-good girl from suburbia who escapes to Los Angeles to be an actress. She meets two guys when she goes to a club with her token lesbian buddy. . . . She can't decide between them, so before long they're shopping and f***ing and living as a threesome. Like great, more Araki outlaws, right? Yeah, except they behave in all these bourgeois ways. The guys get into

this boring hetero antagonistic thing with each other, and Veronica gets all freaked that they won't be able to support her when she gets pregnant. When she runs off to Maui with some earnest [television] movie director named Ernest, you can just hear the queer guys in the audience yellin', "Do it! Do it!" at Abel and Zed as they sit alone together on the couch. But they only hug. Like, hello? (63)

Critics Owen Gleiberman and Emanuel Levy expressed similar disappointment with the film's overall contents. In his *Entertainment Weekly* review, Gleiberman concluded, "Since the movie is actually quite coy about revealing any bedroom details, it gradually loses wattage" (47). Elaborating on such notions, Levy expressed in *Variety*, "What's disappointing about *Splendor* is that Araki shows [no] courage . . . in delineating the kind of relationship that prevails between Abel and Zed when Veronica walks out on them—and they continue to share a household together" (62). Even during the brief scene in which Abel and Zed end up naked in the shower together, everything remains entirely platonic as Abel simply attempts to sober his buddy up so that they can head out to stop Veronica's midnight wedding ceremony.

With *Splendor*, Araki is attempting to rework the classic screwball comedies of the 1930s and 1940s with which he is so smitten. His resulting creation, for example, contains substantial intertextual references to *Design for Living* (Ernst Lubitsch, 1933), a film about two male American artists, one a playwright (played by Fredric March) and the other a painter (played by Gary Cooper), who fall for the same free-spirited woman (played by Miriam Hopkins) and, after she finds herself unable to choose between them, she ends up living with both of them to serve as a critic of their work. It simultaneously contains evidence of intertextual influences from *His Girl Friday* (Howard Hawks, 1940), about a war between the sexes that erupts when a newspaper editor (played by Cary Grant) convinces his star reporter/ex-wife (played by Rosalind Russell) to postpone her marriage to another man in order to cover a big story pertaining to political corruption, as well as *The Philadelphia Story* (George Cukor, 1940), about how a divorced woman who is preparing to remarry (played by Katharine Hepburn) is unexpectedly confronted with having to choose between her past, present, and emergent romantic partners. *Splendor* also contains noteworthy intertextual references to *A Woman Is a Woman* (1961), director Jean-Luc Godard's send-up of Hollywood musical comedies which focuses on an exotic dancer (played by Anna Karina) who very much wishes to have a baby and, after her boyfriend (played by Jean-Claude Brialy) balks at the idea, turns to his best friend (played by Jean-Paul Belmondo) for assistance in the matter, ultimately ending up sleeping with them both.

In interviews, Araki has stated that, with *Splendor*, he intentionally set out to create a *Design for Living*-type of an offering that would end on an optimistic note, serving as his first film with a clearly happy ending ("Designed," par. 12). Because screwball comedy is one of his favorite genres that he learned about in film school, he wanted to create a movie that, like *Bringing Up Baby* and related offerings, explored the deconstruction of manners and social expectations ("Designed," par. 16, 18). He decided to embrace the threeway structure of the film because, as he explains, "In the threeway there is confusion and the element of unpredictability. The dynamic is much more interesting because it is just not a part of what we perceive as Western civilization. . . . Together there are a sort of rules, which they need to figure out. And to some extent that is what the film is about—figuring out how they are going to live" ("Designed," par. 9, 11).

Unlike conventional screwball comedies, which typically end in marriage in order to restore some semblance of the patriarchal social order, Araki's film ends with an ongoing ménage à trois, which is quite atypical in Western society. This is, perhaps, the only innovative or intriguing aspect of his entire creation, however. What Araki seems to have overlooked when deciding to make a screwball comedy in the late 1990s is that screwball comedies in their heyday obtained much of their appeal from the reality that their contents were subject to the repressive restrictions of the Motion Picture Production Code, so they had to covertly communicate controversial romantic and sexual messages in ways that would not be readily identified by film censors. The resulting films, for example, were typically quite adept at utilizing "denial mechanisms" that created ambiguity around potentially transgressive occurrences, suggesting that something transgressive (such as an act of premarital sex) had occurred while providing alternative narrative details or logic that could be utilized simultaneously to deny it (Greene 9; Jacobs 113). The goal of including such mechanisms was to increase the ambiguity as to whether or not taboo actions had actually occurred (Greene 14). Double-meaning gags and instances of double-entendre in dialogue were also utilized commonly in screwball comedies to provide for two or more possible interpretations of identical character actions, one of which was innocent and the other(s) far more risqué (Greene 17-18). *Splendor* contains none of these devices, most likely because it had no need to—in the late 1990s, the sorts of content restrictions common to screwball comedies decades earlier no longer existed; Araki was free to explicitly represent taboo and transgressive narrative developments on-screen to as great an extent as he desired. The fact that he chose not to, especially given the sorts of daring, unapologetic representations of sexual couplings and forms of sexual expression featured in his proceeding films which his fans had come to expect, is one of *Splendor*'s most substantial shortcomings. It results in the film being quite tame and somewhat boring to watch. In addition, as Jan Stuart emphasizes in her *Splendor* review, Araki's film is more a "conventional comedy about unconventional behavior" than a true screwball comedy, because the lovers in screwball comedies historically "wreak havoc without heed or thought to society's mores. They have no choice; it's who they are" (62). In contrast, Araki's central characters in *Splendor*, as Stuart notes, are well aware of the social boundaries they are crossing, and they do so in such subtle, non-threatening ways that they only quite minimally pose any risks at all to society's mores.

Reviewing the film for *The Austin Chronicle*, Marc Savlov referred to it as a "kinder, gentler Gregg Araki film" and noted:

> In fact, almost every aspect of Araki's previous work is missing from *Splendor*. . . . *Splendor*'s dirty little secret? It's *sweet*. In fact, if this movie were any more charming, you'd have to mop the treacle from the floor after each and every screening. . . . The whole project, indeed, is shot through with a giddy, love-puppy sensibility that's wholly unexpected from Araki. No misplaced jism, no beheadings, no penile defenestrations. Araki appears to have traded in his black-clad pop sensibility for a lighter shade of love. (par. 1)

Araki's decidedly uncontroversial, mainstream treatment of *Splendor*'s potentially shocking subject matter ultimately leads the film to become a disappointing, compromised version of *Jules and Jim* (Francois Truffaut, 1962) meets *Three's Company*. At one point in the film, after Mike points out to Veronica that her life with Abel and Zed has indeed become similar to a *Three's Company* rerun, Veronica comments that she found that particular situation comedy, about two single young women and a single young man who end up living together in a Santa Monica apartment in order to make ends meet, to be fairly progressive for its time. It is true that *Three's Company* was relatively progressive on U.S. television in the late 1970s. It is also true that screwball comedies were relatively progressive on the cinematic landscape in the 1930s and 1940s. However, what Araki appears to have failed to recognize is that there is nothing particularly progressive nor interesting about combining their approaches in a film that was made and released in the late 1990s, especially if he did not simultaneously engage in the sorts of genre modification and defiance of cinematic convention for which he had, by then, become well-known. Lacking entirely in *Splendor* are the hallmarks of Araki's trademark post-punk style—for example, there are no provocative images of non-heterosexual sexual activity, there are no acts of visceral violence, there is no defiance of cinematic convention (with the possible exception of the film's ménage-à-trois ending), and there is no unapologetic foregrounding of a range of human sexualities and sexual practices that have historically been marginalized by mainstream society. Also missing are Araki's expected inclusion of bizarre, marginal characters who populate a seemingly surrealistic Los Angeles (despite the reality that all three of the film's central characters derive their somewhat limited incomes by working in different aspects of the Hollywood entertainment industry), the intentional lack of traditional commercial appeal, the intentional refusal to take the film and its subject matter too seriously, and the utilization of such cinematic attributes to make a powerful statement about non-heterosexuality and/or non-heterosexual individuals living in the age of AIDS. As a result, *Splendor* ends up feeling like an unnecessarily mainstream film that has been made by an entirely different director.

Concluding Observations

When punk music emerged in Britain and the United States in the mid 1970s, it represented a distinct form of cultural production that encouraged a potent spirit of anarchy and disorder and challenged hegemonic social expectations. Within just a few years, however, the punk aesthetic had been substantially incorporated into mainstream culture, stripping it of the majority of its subversive potential and contributing significantly to its rapid demise (Hebdige 94-96). A similar phenomenon occurred with regard to Gregg Araki and his post-punk filmmaking style over the decade of the 1990s, as his various character types and their on-screen actions became far more tame as investor expectations for the financial returns of his films continued to grow. In a (largely failed) attempt to attract a larger audience and generate more impressive box-office returns, the director began to tone down the extreme visuals and storylines that were so essential to the effective application of his post-punk authorial style. About this process of incorporation into the mainstream, which he realizes is frequently essential to achieving commercial success, Araki has utilized the metaphor of an amoeba spreading wildly and absorbing everything around it, pushing further and further toward the margins and steadily drifting toward him (Chang 50).

Following the releases of both *Nowhere* and *Splendor*, numerous fans and critics alike believed that Araki's career, if he would actually continue to have one, had entered a state of terminal decline (Zion, "Truth" F14). The director who, just a few years earlier, was characterized as "an anarchic filmmaker in the tradition of Vigo and Pasolini, showing us areas of human behavior and transgression that test our limits as an audience" (Severson, par. 4), had apparently disappeared, being replaced by a far more tame and uninteresting filmmaker with decidedly mainstream aspirations. When asked, shortly after *Splendor* was released, about the types of films he would like to make in the future, Araki responded that he would enjoy making either a musical or a fifty-million-dollar action film ("Designed," par. 24). This reality is particularly distressing because it pertains to a formerly intriguing independent director who personally stated, after being catapulted to New Queer Cinema notoriety following the release of *The Living End* in 1992, "It's really important that my films go way out there. One of the things that really bothers me about a lot of independent films is that they don't take any chances formally, politically, or in choice of content" ("Rebellious," par. 9).

By the end of the 1990s, it had become quite clear that Araki had lost focus of his original filmmaking goals as well as the hallmarks of his post-punk authorial style. Perhaps the most positive thing that could be said about the resulting state of his filmmaking career at that point was several critics had noted that *Nowhere* and *Splendor* continued to develop the distinctive visual style of his films, even if their contents were no longer particularly groundbreaking, culturally relevant, nor inherently interesting (Levi, "Nowhere" 66; Satuloff 92).

Chapter 5
Reestablishing Relevancy with
Mysterious Skin

At the start of the new millennium, Gregg Araki's filmmaking career appeared to be in shambles. As one critic noted, toward the end of the 1990s, the director "continued to trade on shock value, but with diminishing artistic returns" (Zion, "Truth" F14). Another critic stated that, over time, many individuals were likely "put off by something else that does, admittedly, have the potential to hurt ticket sales: the fact that [a] film was made by Gregg Araki" (Porter F15). Yet another critic emphasized that Araki's "highly publicized off-screen romance with [Kathleen Robertson] strained the GLBT community's acceptance of the auteur as a 'serious filmmaker' of gay-themed films" (Dossi 65).

Certainly, in the aftermath of the release of *Splendor*, Araki's filmmaking career had, to say the least, become a bit enigmatic. Accordingly, it raised noteworthy questions about what loyal fans should make of an auteur director whose most recent offering differed so substantially from his preceding body of cinematic work. Because he was widely regarded as a noteworthy auteur during the decade of the 1990s, Araki was expected by his fans to continue to explore in his later films the same types of themes he had consistently explored in his preceding ones for, as Jean Renoir once noted, the most noteworthy auteur directors typically spend their entire lives making just one film—as in the same basic film over and over again—with certain variations and permutations that become evident through the process of viewing their entire oeuvre (Wollen 575). Andrew Sarris echoed that same notion, in his early articulation of auteur theory, when he emphasized that an auteur director is most readily identifiable by the consistency of interior meaning that exists within his or her various creations, which becomes evi-

dent through the pattern that is established over the course of several films
(563). As such, Araki's auteurist status became endangered when he turned
his back almost entirely on the thematic preoccupations of his preceding
works, in an attempt to lure a larger audience, with *Splendor.*

When an auteur director with an "outsider sensibility," such as Araki,
makes a substantial narrative and representational shift toward the "mainstream," he or she risks alienating his or her entire core following, especially
when that director's resulting cinematic creations become virtually unrecog-
nizable by the largely queer audience that embraced them from the beginning. Admittedly, the outrage surrounding the AIDS pandemic mellowed
substantially over the decade of the 1990s, and acceptance of non-
heterosexual sexual identities continued to grow during that same period,
both of which naturally had at least some impact on Araki's filmmaking
choices as his career progressed. The director's romantic relationship with a
woman, who performed in *Nowhere* and became the star of *Splendor,* also
played a role. Nevertheless, given Araki's prior status as a leading director
of the New Queer Cinema, his remaining loyal fans reasonably still expected
the auteur, at a minimum, to embrace controversial subject matter and non-
heterosexual themes in his films—both of which were lacking in his seventh
feature—and to continue to incorporate his post-punk authorial style. If
Araki wished to redeem himself and reestablish his cultural relevancy in the
eyes of his fans, it appeared that he would have to return to his filmmaking
roots in whatever offering became his eighth feature film, if indeed there
would ever be one. The years went by without a new Araki film. Then, in
late 2004, *Mysterious Skin,* a story of self-discovery as two teenage boys
come to terms with the reality of having been sexually abused by their Little
League coach years earlier and its psychological aftermath, premiered at the
Venice Film Festival before going on to impress fans and critics across the
globe.

Eliminating the Enigma by Embracing the Mysterious

Mysterious Skin, Araki's first screenplay adaptation (from the acclaimed
novel by Scott Heim), represented the auteur director's successful attempts
to reestablish his cinematic and cultural relevancy in relation to the expectations of his core audience as well as the approaches and subject matter of
contemporary queer cinema. It unflinchingly deals with the subject matter of
pedophilia, prostitution, and rape as it presents the stories of Kansas resi-
dents Neil McCormick (played by Chase Ellison as a child and Joseph
Gordon-Levitt as a teenager) and Brian Lackey (played by George Webster
as a child and Brady Corbet as a teenager), whose lives are inherently in-

tertwined as a result of the sexual abuse they encountered at the hands of their Little League coach (played by Bill Sage) when they were both only eight years old, over the course of a decade (from 1981 to 1991). As he matures, the cocky Neil becomes a hustler who, by having sex with older gay men, seeks the same sense of comfort and status of being special that he derived from his consensual (or so he maintains throughout the film) sexual encounters with the coach years earlier. In contrast, the shy and reclusive Brian has blocked out his memories of such encounters entirely and has replaced them with the belief that he has experienced firsthand encounters with space aliens, instead.

Following his first sexual encounter with the coach, Brian blacks out for several hours, ultimately waking up, with a nosebleed, in the crawl space of his family's home. In the weeks (and ultimately years) that follow, he wets his bed occasionally, and he regularly experiences nightmares and nosebleeds. Following another sexual encounter with the coach on Halloween night a few years later, Brian blacks out again. Over time, he ends up convincing himself that he must have been abducted by aliens during those missing hours of his life, which helps to explain the dreams he continues to have about being "probed" by another being. Neil, on the other hand, apparently realized that he was gay at the age of eight, and as a result he welcomed the predatory sexual encounters with the coach, whom he found to be quite attractive, similar to the images of naked lifeguards, cowboys, and firemen he had secretly viewed in issues of his mother's *Playgirl* magazines. At that same age, Neil also watched his mother having sex with her Marlboro-Man-looking boyfriend—which later became "his type"—on the swing set in their yard, masturbating all the while. Having been the star of the team and the coach's favorite player, Neil felt honored that the coach picked him to be with on a recurring basis, even if the two of them occasionally involved other teammates in their sexual activities. A decade later, Neil still romanticizes his encounters with the coach and recalls them with a combined aura of childhood innocence and nostalgia. Their competing realities are summarized quite succinctly in the film's tagline, which states, "Two boys. One can't remember. The other can't forget."

For much of the film, Brian and Neil's stories run parallel to each other; it is not until the closing sequence that they intersect and Neil helps Brian to remember what actually occurred between the two boys and Coach one night so long ago. Before that intersection occurs, Neil begins hustling at a park in his hometown of Hutchinson and eventually continues that "profession," during some of the darkest days of the AIDS pandemic, in New York City, where he joins his childhood friend and soul mate Wendy (played by Riley McGuire as a child and Michelle Trachtenberg as a teenager), who moved there a year earlier. Once Neil joins Wendy in the city and begins to turn tricks, she reminds him that they're not in Kansas anymore, referring at once to the reality that he needs to engage in safe sex and grow up. In contrast, Brian continues to live at home with his mother, jotting down recollections of his recurring dreams and beginning classes at the local community college. While watching a television special pertaining to UFO abductions, he learns of Avalyn Friesen (played by Mary Lynn Rajskub), a thirty-two-year-old, unmarried secretary who lives with her farmer father in a town located just half an hour away. Avalyn claims to have discovered, through the process of hypnotic regression, that she was abducted by aliens nearly two dozen times, beginning at the age of six. Naturally, the woman's experiences and close proximity intrigue Brian, who writes her a letter and ultimately befriends her. Together, Avalyn attempts to help Brian make sense of what likely happened to him on the nights that he experienced missing time while a child. She shows him a scar on her thigh, where she believes that aliens have implanted a tracking device, and she adds that Brian's nosebleeds suggest that is where his own tracking device was implanted, in order to avoid a scar. She listens to the details of his dreams, like a detective following the clues. She attempts to assist Brian in his pursuit of sexual discovery (although he rejects her advances, because they unknowingly remind him of his experiences with the coach). She also discovers the name "N. McCormick" on the back of a framed photograph of Brian's Little League team, which takes him in search of the other boy who appears regularly in his dreams. His efforts lead him to the McCormick home on the day that Neil has departed for New York City, where Brian ends up befriending Neil's closest male friend, Eric (played by Jeff Licon), who clearly has an unrequited crush on Neil and is saddened when he is left behind in Kansas. Brian and Eric then begin spending increasing amounts of time together, both in and out of their community college classes. Eric informs Neil of their interactions by postcard, describing Brian as strangely asexual and noting that Brian and Neil once played in Little League together. Eric adds that Brian believes he and Neil were once abducted by space aliens together.

Ultimately, Neil and Brian's defensive fantasies are abolished when Eric introduces them to one another upon Neil's holiday return to Kansas and he drives them to Coach's old house. As he approaches the front door, Brian is struck by the blue light on the porch, which matches the shade that he has been associating in his memories and dreams for years with the interior of an alien spaceship. Left alone by Eric, Neil and Brian enter the home on Christmas Eve through an unlocked window, directly into Coach's old bedroom (which is now another family's nursery), as carolers can be heard singing down the street. In the kitchen, Neil is disappointed to find that the cabinets are no longer stocked with snacks, so he devours a cookie from a snowman cookie jar. Settling on the living room sofa, Brian informs Neil that he has sought him out because he would like to dream about something different for a change. Accordingly, Neil begins to tell him about his own experiences that summer with Coach, and he proceeds to share the details about the night that Coach, following a rained-out baseball game, brought Brian back to the house with them. As on the other occasions when Coach brought home another boy, Neil was used by him as a prop, to convince the onlooker that the sexual acts being initiated were a type of fun game. Neil explains that he kissed Brian first, to get his mouth all shiny and wet for Coach, who kissed him next. Then, Coach and Neil removed Brian's clothes. Neil went down on Brian briefly, followed by Coach. Afterwards, the boys played the "five-dollar game." On that evening, it required Neil, and then Brian, to fist Coach, all the way up to their elbows, in order to receive a five-dollar bill. Immediately thereafter, as Coach and Neil were getting Brian dressed, Brian fell face first to the floor, which caused his nose to start bleeding. Then, they drove Brian home and left him in his driveway. By the time Neil finishes revealing the details of that abusive evening, Brian once again has a bloody nose on the sofa, and he begins to shake uncontrollably. Neil holds him tight in their womb-like setting, attempting to comfort him. The film concludes with carolers at the door singing "Silent Night," over-shadowed by a voiceover from Neil explaining how he wanted to tell Brian that everything would now be alright (but he knew that wasn't true, and he found himself unable to speak anyway), that he wished there was a way they could go back and undo what had happened to them in the past, and that, like two angels, they could both simply leave this world behind at that moment and magically disappear.

Clearly, with *Mysterious Skin*, Araki once again embraced his penchant for exploring controversial subject matter in boundary-pushing ways. In part, his representation of pedophilia in this film is off-putting to many viewers because it blatantly portrays Neil, at the very early age of eight, as being a decidedly (homo)sexual being (Ide F9). At the same time, his approach is further noteworthy because, unlike other films such as *Happiness* (Todd Solondz, 1998) and *The Woodsman* (Nicole Kassell, 2004) that take viewers into the minds of the abusers, Araki's offering takes viewers on a decade-long, psychologically complex and devastating journey into the lives and minds of the abused individuals themselves, in addition to portraying their victimizer relatively sympathetically (Dossi 65; Ide F9) as "at once the predator who stole Neil's innocence, the father he never had, and the great love of his life" (Green and Goode 82). As James Christopher emphasized in his discussion of the film, based on his interview with the director:

> In short, Neil is not the tabloid image of an abused child, and the coach "is
> not this weird evil man who pitches up in a van out of nowhere. He's your

next-door neighbor," Araki says, "the most normal guy in the world. It's in the story that Neil is gay at an early age and attracted to the coach, but I feel he is the most damaged individual in the film. Yes, there are some things in the movie that open your eyes, that shed light on something so taboo that people don't want to talk about it. But if people don't want to acknowledge uncomfortable truths then abuse will always happen." (F14)

Perhaps surprisingly, given the unapologetic representations of Araki's preceding offerings, there are no actual scenes of childhood sexual abuse in this work; the sexual scenes featuring Coach and the young boys have been carefully storyboarded and edited to suggest what has occurred while protecting the child actors from experiencing anything inappropriate, with the end result of making their implied actions all the more haunting and provocative because they are mentally rather than visually graphic (Esther 44; LaSalle E5; Lee, par. 8; Seguin F17). Nevertheless, as Michael Koresky points out in his *Film Comment* review, in typical Araki fashion, "there's still enough aggressive sex to scare off the straights" (73).

From Page to Screen: Reflections on the Adaptation Process

Given the film's subject matter and representational approaches, Araki, like many other people, was surprised to find that *Mysterious Skin* was embraced as a critical success and ended up being included on several critics' lists of the top-ten films of 2004 (Christopher F14; Hays, *View* 37; Zion, "Child" L4). In addition, numerous critics regard *Mysterious Skin* as being the best film of his career (Chonin E1), at least in part because its transgressive nature enables it very effectively to "question the unquestionable" by showing, in the words of Araki, "hidden territory that happens every day in our society, but that society tries to pretend doesn't happen" (Seguin F17). He should not have been so surprised. In large part, the success of the film is bolstered by the source material upon which it is based—Heim's semiautobiographical novel is quite powerful and engaging, to the extent that it brought Araki to tears the first time he read it (Christopher F14). The director has said that, because the novel had such a tremendous emotional impact on him and its contents haunted him for several years, he knew that *Mysterious Skin* would likely one day become his first film based on another person's material if he ever decided to move in that direction (Esther 44; Lee, par. 5).

Araki's decision to adapt Heim's novel for the screen was somewhat unexpected, most notably because all of his preceding feature films had been the products of his own imagination. By the time he released *Nowhere* and *Splendor*, however, it was becoming increasingly clear that Araki was running low on personal creativity, to the extent that he had begun to release increasingly tame and comparatively uninteresting cinematic works that appealed neither to mainstream audiences nor his remaining core of New Queer Cinema fans. On the surface, his decision to base his next film on another author's work would appear to call Araki's status as an auteur into question, because it is commonly assumed that each film released by an auteur director is primarily the result of that individual's own creative processes, with the director serving as "the dominant personality who has made that effort cohere and whose force and creative vision have chiefly shaped the finished film" (Bywater and Sobchack 53). Nevertheless, because Araki personally served as the adaptor of Heim's novel in his role as screenwriter on this project, he retained a substantial degree of agency as a primary creative force who shaped the finished film, making complex decisions about which narrative developments to feature or eliminate, and how to treat those that made the cut, in his efforts to reduce a nearly three-hundred-page book into an approximately one-hundred-minute film. In addition, he took comfort in the fact that he and Heim are similar in noteworthy ways—for example, they are both gay, they are the same age, they like the same types of music, and they are creative individuals with an interest in telling stories about outsiders (Esther 45)—and he has indicated that he loved Heim's source material as much as he loves entities that are entirely of his own creation (Hays, *View* 42). In a very real sense, then, *Mysterious Skin*, in both its subject matter and its treatment of that subject matter, is a Gregg Araki story through and through.

About the process of adapting Heim's novel for the screen, Araki has stated, "When I was doing the adaptation, it was important to me that the film be very faithful to the book because I love the story so much, and I thought it was such a powerful story and such a beautiful story. . . . I had the book with me the whole time I was writing" (Lee, par. 21). It is perhaps unsurprising, therefore, that Araki's resulting screenplay does indeed remain quite faithful to its original source material in numerous ways.

For example, one very noteworthy aspect that stands out from the first few chapters of Heim's novel is the degree to which Coach's apartment is designed to serve as a child magnet, replete with casual furnishings (e.g., beanbag chairs), tempting treats (e.g., snack foods of all kinds), and appealing diversions (e.g., all of the latest Atari video games). It is also a welcoming, laid-back environment in which nothing that grown-ups typically frown upon—including the occasional food fight—appears to be off limits. Araki's film captures these same elements and their various appeals, from the viewpoint of a child, perfectly, which enables Coach to seduce Neil rather efficiently. To get Neil alone for the first time, the coach informs Neil's mother (played by Elisabeth Shue), after his team's first win, that he is taking his players out to celebrate. Instead, he picks up only Neil and they spend the day together in a simulated date, complete with a movie (an R-rated slasher flick that Neil chooses) and dinner (pizza, which they pick up and take back to the coach's home). Immediately thereafter, while they play Atari video games together, the coach inadvertently distracts Neil, which causes the boy to mess up; Neil utters a profane word as a result. This appears to turn the coach on, as he grabs a nearby tape recorder, encourages Neil to belch into its microphone loudly, and asks him to repeat the same profane word several times. Seconds later, the coach grabs a Polaroid camera and encourages Neil to strike a variety of playful poses; as he does so, he instructs Neil to open his mouth very wide, inserts his thumb (as a penis symbol) atop the boy's tongue, and snaps the picture to serve later as a fantasy device. It is not until their next night alone together at Coach's home, however, that anything explicitly sexual occurs between the two. During that encounter, Coach shows Neil the photo album containing all of the Polaroids he shot of him and then, when Neil indicates that he is hungry, he leads the boy to the kitchen and opens a cabinet, which is extremely well stocked with snacks. Neil is drawn to the cabinet's assortment of miniature boxes of cereal, at least in part because his mother refuses to buy them, claiming that they are a waste of money. He becomes upset when he spills his box of Corn Pops accidentally while opening it, but, rather than getting angry as Neil expected, Coach appears to be amused. The two proceed to open several of the additional small boxes and toss their contents into the air as well, creating a rainbow of cereal bits on the floor. It is then that Coach makes his move. Pushing Neil gently down to the floor, Coach rests his head on Neil's chest and then moves in for a kiss. What follows remains concealed from the viewer; however, when the encounter has concluded, Coach reassures Neil that he liked it and that it is okay that he did so. Araki's dialogue and visuals (especially the image of colorful cereal bits falling down endlessly upon Neil from above, which he recalls in brief flashbacks elsewhere in the film) effectively convey both the substance and mood of Heim's descriptions of these same events, making their effect on the viewer all the more disconcerting as he or she vicariously experiences everything that the young victim of pedophilia is experiencing.

Neil's close relationship with Wendy is another important aspect of Heim's novel that Araki captures quite effectively on film, albeit with a tremendous amount of compression. To do so, the director vividly brings to life the novel's sequence from Halloween 1983, when Neil was ten years old and Wendy was eleven, during which their bond became solidified. In Araki's film, the pair "kidnap" a mentally handicapped boy while he is trick-or-treating, force him to lie on the ground and hold bottle rockets in his lips, ignite the fireworks, and launch them into the night sky. Immediately thereafter, upon discovering their victim's bloody mouth and splintered lips, Wendy panics, fearing that the boy is going to tell on them. Neil responds that there are things they can do to get him on their side. He then proceeds to masturbate the boy before progressing to give him a blowjob. Wendy looks on in shock, realizing simultaneously that Neil is gay and that he has also been the victim of childhood sexual abuse. In voiceover, as the sequence draws to a close, Neil emphasizes that the evening's events bound him and Wendy together forever. Araki's decision to focus on this particular scene, for the sake of efficiency, was quite insightful. In the novel, Heim is able to reveal the bonds of their relationship far more gradually, as Wendy discovers that her initial crush on Neil is doomed to failure because he is queer, which he reveals one day during their middle school recess by hypnotizing a straight male student, lying on top of him, and kissing him before the boy snaps out of his trance, to the shock of everyone else around them. Thereafter, Wendy remained impressed with her newfound friend's willingness to stick out as an outsider—such as when he pointed out, during a sex-ed presentation of a penis entering a vagina, that not everyone fucks like that—because her association with Neil made her appear all the more interesting and alternative to others. Although these sorts of additional compelling details are glossed over entirely in Araki's film, the screenwriter-director ended up featuring the most ideal sequence contained in Heim's novel that conveys the depth and foundation of Neil and Wendy's relationship in the most efficient possible way.

Yet another very noteworthy way that Araki's film remains faithful to Heim's source material is in its representation of Neil's need to remain in control, once he begins hustling, whenever he is with his various johns. While hustling in Kansas, Neil consistently takes great pride in retaining a high degree of control with the older men who pay for his services, making it very clear what he is, and is not, willing to do for cash. His level of confidence in this regard similarly extends to his first hustling experience in New York City, during which he is further pleased to discover that the going rate for his services is one hundred twenty dollars an hour, up from just fifty in Kansas. His sense of control is reduced just a bit during this scene, however, in an effective example of subtle foreshadowing of what will follow for Neil in this "profession," when the man commands him to fuck him up the ass but insists that he wear a condom while doing so. When Neil, who has not been engaging regularly in safe sex and recently recovered from a case of crabs, appears shocked as well as entirely uncertain how to put one on, the man does so for him.

His second sexual encounter for pay in the big city goes quite differently, however. As his customer undresses, Neil becomes disconcerted when he notices that the man's entire torso is covered with KS lesions. Although all the john requires is that the naked Neil rub his back (because he needs to be touched) and later masturbate while he watches, the encounter leaves Neil in a disillusioned state, as he runs through the city streets back to Wendy's apartment. Once there, he explains that this was the first time in his entire life that he was bothered by the act of hustling, in which he has been engaging in a failed attempt to feel the special way that he felt when he was eight years old and (according to his recollection at least) Coach truly loved him.

It is Neil's next sexual encounter for pay that causes him to dangerously lose all control. Just hours before he is to head home to Kansas for Christmas, using the plane ticket sent to him by his mother, Neil is picked up by a gruff man while he is walking down the street. Once inside the man's Brighton Beach bedroom, the man orders Neil to snort cocaine and, after snorting the rest himself, commands Neil to strip while he does the same. When Neil moves a bit too slowly, the man pushes him down on the bed and tears off his pants. Referring to Neil repeatedly as "slut," he then orders Neil to open wide and suck his dick. When Neil hesitates, the man slaps him hard across the face, grabs him by the head, forces him to his knees, and again orders him to suck him. Moments later, as Neil is complying, the man looks down at him and spits in his face. Throwing Neil onto the bed, he announces that "slut" knows what's coming next. Neil protests, saying that there are some things he doesn't do and that he needs to take a piss; he slides out from under the john and seeks refuge in the nearby bathroom, locking its door with an old-fashioned hook-shaped latch that fits into a mounted eyehole. Seconds later, he watches in horror as the man uses a butter knife to unlock the door and, after a moment of silence, bursts into the room and uses the knife to hit Neil squarely in the face, knocking him into the bathtub. He then lifts Neil's legs in the air and rapes him brutally, calling him a "slut" with every thrust and beating Neil in the face nearly a dozen times with a bottle of baby shampoo as Neil's blood runs down the drain, in a manner reminiscent of the extremely violent beating of the drug dealer with a Campbell's Tomato Soup can in Araki's *Nowhere*. The significance of the baby shampoo must not be overlooked, as this scene represents the turning point in Neil's life when his childhood innocence is finally shattered and he stops romanticizing his sexual interactions with Coach from a decade earlier, beginning to see them as abusive rather than loving for the first time. Emotionally, this scene is at least as brutal as the one in *Twist* (Jacob Tierney, 2003), a queer retelling of the Dickens classic, in which a young man refers to his own hustler brother (played by Nick Stahl) as a "whore" and forces the boy to give him a blowjob in exchange for much-needed cash. Both physically and emotionally, it is nearly as brutal as the concluding sequence of *Skin and Bone* (Everett Lewis, 1996), during which a bound-and-gagged hustler (played by B. Wyatt), who has just had a huge nightstick shoved violently up his anus, is unwittingly murdered by a fellow hustler (played by Alan Boyce) with whom he is engaged in a cop fantasy for a client after their pimp replaces a fake gun filled with blanks with a real one filled with bullets, and the bound hustler witnesses that exchange but is unable to adequately communicate in time what he has just seen. Although these scenes with the various New York City johns are directly inspired by the pages of Heim's novel, it is nevertheless quite a feat for Araki to vividly and so convincingly capture on-screen all of the conflicting emotions, disconcerting locations, and compelling character types that had previously been communicated solely in words on a page.

In adapting Heim's novel to create this intriguing film, Araki hoped to show that children everywhere, even in the seemingly more innocent Midwest, experience feelings of vulnerability and insecurity and, as a result, can fall prey to the dangers that lurk in today's world ("Outspoken," par. 6). He also hoped to show the complex emotional journeys that are typically experienced by victims of pedophilia as well as by their abusers. As Araki explains, "This is not a black-and-white narrative. Scott [Heim] was very adept at crafting human and nuanced characters. Even in the scenes of abuse, the coach and johns have human frailties and flaws. That makes the story more disturbing and truthful. I wanted to tell what was an uncompromising book in an uncompromising way. I did not want it to be a TV movie of the week" (Teeman F19).

In his quest to translate an uncompromising book into his uncompromising film, however, Araki nevertheless made certain decisions during the adaptation process that diverge substantially from Heim's source material, which enabled him to put his own spin on the narrative that ultimately unfolds on-screen. One of the most readily identifiable examples of such differences occurs early in the film, as the eight-year-old Brian, his sister, and his mother unquestionably glimpse a huge blue spaceship in the night sky. In contrast, Heim's novel intentionally leaves doubt as to whether the group of blue lights these three individuals (along with a male work associate of Brian's mother, whose presence suggests that she may actually be involved in an extramarital romantic relationship) witnessed hovering in the night sky actually were a UFO. Although the change may not appear to be especially significant (and Araki's version admittedly is far more intriguing to view on-screen), it strongly lends credence to the possibility that Brian may indeed have been abducted by space aliens when he was quite young, throwing the viewer further off the track of what actually has occurred in his past. For what transpires between Brian and the coach when Brian is just eight years old, as well as on Halloween two years later, remains concealed from the viewer (who only learns the distressing details as Brian simultaneously discovers them when he is a teenager), and Araki is a big fan of using aliens metaphorically to make provocative statements about conditions that are commonly experienced in our everyday world (Esther 45).

Another substantial difference between the contents of Heim's novel and Araki's film involves the degree to which Brian's close relationships with both his mother and his sister get lost in the translation from page to screen. In Heim's novel, Brian's mother is the individual who provided great comfort to him by bathing him tenderly on the night he blacked out for several hours before waking up in the crawl space of his family's home. Despite her busy work schedule, she also carved out plenty of time to spend with her son and provide emotional support to him, such as by taking him out for ice cream, accompanying him on a daylong mother–son fishing excursion, listening to his theory of how he had been abducted by aliens, and surprising him with a special journal in which to record the details of his memories and dreams. In addition, Brian's sister, Deborah, is the individual who helped Brian to come to terms with the reality of his blackouts when he was young, spent countless hours hanging out and playing games with him on the roof of their home, sold watermelons with him at a roadside stand, attended church with him each week, occasionally allowed him to hang out with her female friends, danced with him joyfully on the night that their father left their mother for good, and regarded herself as one of Brian's closest friends. In Araki's film, however, these close bonds are largely nonexistent. Although Brian's mother (played by Lisa Long) appears regularly throughout the film, with the exception of the early scene in which she bathes her eight-year-old son at the end of his traumatic evening, she comes across primarily as a somewhat distant and sarcastic individual, rather than the nurturer of Heim's novel. For example, she makes fun of the televised UFO special that Brian invites her to watch with him, and she constantly rolls her eyes and utters derogatory comments whenever Avalyn telephones Brian. Deborah (played by Rachael Kraft as a child and Kelly Kruger as a college student) is barely in the film at all—she is a minor part of the familial backdrop when Brian is a child and briefly returns home from college for Christmas a decade later, when she hugs her brother and affectionately rubs his neck to indicate that there is some sort of warm bond between them. The end result of these changes is that Brian comes across as being a far more isolated and marginalized individual in Araki's film, which solidifies his "outsider" status (an attribute common in all of Araki's films) and serves to explain the strength of the bond that he ultimately forms with Avalyn.

Neil's relationship with Eric is quite different in the novel and the film, as well. In Heim's novel, during the months before Neil departed Kansas for New York, it is clear that he and Eric made out and had sex together on several occasions—and that it was actually Neil who initiated their first sexual encounter—which helps to explain the resulting degree of Eric's romantic longing for Neil. It is primarily because Neil's Coach-fixation has led him to be attracted most substantially to older men that their potential romantic relationship never fully materializes. In contrast, in Araki's film, Eric is portrayed as a lovesick puppy following endlessly on the heels of Neil, who seems to callously take advantage of his companion's unspoken affection (of which he is evidently aware). Neil insensitively allows Eric to pick him up at the park each day upon the conclusion of his hustling activities, and he openly discusses his attraction to, and sexual exploits with, other men in front of him. On one occasion, as Eric pulls into Neil's driveway, Neil gazes deeply into Eric's eyes and smiles coyly, as if a kiss is about to occur, but then abruptly exits the vehicle. On another occasion, after a night of heavy drinking, Neil brings Eric back to his bedroom, throws himself down spread eagle on the bed—and then informs Eric that there is a gay porn video in the VCR if he wants to jack off. As a result of these differences, the Neil of Araki's movie comes across as being a far more heartless and highly insensitive individual than the Neil of Heim's novel, which causes Eric to come across as a bit more pathetic as a result of his devotion to such an individual. These changes cause audience members to feel a bit less compassion for Araki's Neil as he pursues his self-destructive path by positioning him even more strongly as an aloof and detached outsider. They also make the scene in which Neil pulls out his penis and implores Eric to kneel down and take a close look at it—during which Eric discovers that Neil is suffering from a bad case of crabs—seem all the more callous and cruel.

Accordingly, while Araki's treatment and compression of Heim's source material is extremely effective at capturing the novel's overall essence and translating it to the screen, it simultaneously enabled the screenwriter-director to make a number of significant modifications that helped to make the resulting story his own, and another clear example of a "Gregg Araki movie." The end result is a compelling work that maximizes the outsider status of both central characters in relation to their ever-present feelings of teenage alienation and resulting emotional needs. As one critic remarked:

> From the hyperbolic, pop saturation of its images to its theme of pretty young things wrestling with their place in the world, it's an Araki film through and through, but the story—adapted from Scott Heim's 1996 book of the same name—is tightly wound and has a stabilizing effect on Araki's typically erratic and high-strung visual style, which tends to flail around aimlessly when it has no narrative momentum to hold on to. . . . For Araki, then, *Mysterious Skin* spells progress. (Gonzalez, par. 1)

Similarly, another critic noted, "It's certainly not going to sit well with some audiences, but to my mind Araki's unflinching approach to taboo subjects has never worked better than it does in this excellent film" (Zion, "Child" L4).

Perhaps even more importantly with regard to the critical success of the film, however, *Mysterious Skin* represents the return of this auteur director to embracing controversial subject matter and non-heterosexual themes and exploring them using his post-punk authorial style. The hallmarks of Araki's signature style are, to the delight of the director's loyal fans, once again readily evident in *Mysterious Skin*. The various scenes featuring Neil's sexual interactions with Coach as well as his various johns, both in Kansas and New York City, provide provocative images of non-heterosexual sexual activity. An incident during which a redneck in a pickup truck aims a loaded shotgun at Neil and Eric, calls them "faggots," and prepares to shoot them for being queer, coupled with Neil's unexpected rape in Brighton Beach, provide the seemingly random acts of violence common to Araki's films. With this film, although Araki returns to foregrounding outsiders as well as space aliens in a story pertaining to teen alienation during the age of AIDS (as he had with *Nowhere*), he simultaneously defies cinematic convention with regard to both the content and form of the subgenre of the teen film, and also with regard to linearity as *Mysterious Skin* features two seemingly isolated storylines that run parallel for the majority of the film before intersecting to achieve an especially powerful climax. By exploring the phenomenon of man–boy love (as Neil regards his interactions with Coach), gay prostitution, as well as the sexual act of fisting in relation to two gay male characters, the film foregrounds various human sexualities and sexual practices that have historically been marginalized by mainstream society. Like most other Araki films, this one includes lengthy scenes that play out in real time in order to heighten their emotionality, most notably the concluding scene in which Neil informs Brian of the missing details from his memories. Although this film does not feature the inclusion of bizarre street people and other marginal characters who populate a seemingly surrealistic Los Angeles (because it is set in Kansas and New York City), it nevertheless features the equivalent of them in the form of the potentially marginal characters of Brian and Avalyn—who might come across as somewhat pathetic misfits rather than well-rounded and compelling individuals in the hands of another director—as well as the various johns that Neil tricks with throughout the film. Without question, given that it is a film about pedophilia and its psychological ramifications, *Mysterious Skin* inherently contains an intentional lack of traditional commercial appeal; as one film buyer stated in the presence of Araki, "I think it's a tough film . . . from a commercial point of view. . . . For commercial terms, I just think it's too tough" (Pomeranz, par. 3). Finally, despite the film's extremely serious subject matter, it nevertheless refuses to take itself and its subject matter entirely seriously, such as by featuring a campy haunted house scene, a fantasy-like scene in an abandoned drive-in theater parking lot during which Neil and Wendy hear the "voice of God" through a speaker as snow begins to fall seemingly magically all around them, a playful scene during which Neil receives a blowjob from a john while he is working as a sportscaster during a baseball game, and the presence of the character of Eric, who adds levity to the surrounding on-screen developments with his consistently upbeat personality and ever-changing hair color and makeup.

"My movies are always about outsiders and amorphous sexuality," Araki has stated, "so [*Mysterious Skin*] was an ideal film for me" (Chonin E1). With the release of this offering, therefore, Gregg Araki's filmmaking career no longer appeared to be enigmatic. In fact, and instead, it appeared to have come full circle, with *Mysterious Skin* representing the impressive "maturation of the director's storytelling abilities" (Dossi 65) as well as the most emotionally involving film of his entire career.

Concluding Observations

Surprisingly, despite its controversial and potentially taboo subject matter which one critic characterized as "not for the fainthearted, the squeamish, or the inflexibly decent" (Thomson WE34), *Mysterious Skin* went on to become a hit with both alternative and mainstream audiences alike. "The last thing I thought about in making it was that it would be my most accessible or commercial movie," Araki has said, "yet of all my films, it's had the most mainstream embrace. Even *People* magazine liked it. That's kind of strange for me" (Chonin E1). A big part of the film's widespread appeal is that it addresses the topic of pedophilia, a deleterious phenomenon that is quite common—affecting approximately one out of every four children around the world (Esther 45)—yet rarely blatantly spoken about, while at the same time acknowledging the "reality of sexual self-awareness in children" (Zion, "Truth" F14). As critic Desson Thomson explained in *The Washington Post*, "In the context of Araki's film, something else is happening. The eight-year-old Neil, who has a big crush on his coach, has partly engineered this seduction, and he's perhaps even more lost in the passionate moment than [Coach] Heider" (WE34). Araki himself echoed such notions when he stated:

> The fact that Neil is a very young age and is gay and has desires made the story more realistic, because to me, people who have had this experience in their life come up to me after the movie and tell me it's really, really truthful. And that is what makes *Mysterious Skin* so unsettling. It's much more reassuring to watch a movie where your innocent kid is out playing in the

playground and is whisked away in a van and it's all black-and-white and terrible. (Zion, "Truth" F14)

As demonstrated in the preceding chapter, by the end of the 1990s, Araki's post-punk authorial style appeared to be at risk of disappearing entirely as the director sought out larger audiences and more mainstream acceptance and began to embrace less daring subject matter and representational approaches as a result. If that had indeed become the case, and Araki had not reversed those trends with the release of *Mysterious Skin*, it would have been quite difficult to know what to make of such developments or, perhaps even more importantly, how they would affect his remaining queer audience. The reality that Araki instead utilized his post-punk authorial style to create the most mature offering of his entire career, one that once again embraced controversial subject matter and non-heterosexual themes, proved to be a refreshing move in his efforts to reestablish cinematic and cultural relevancy in relation to the expectations of his core audience as well as the approaches and subject matter of contemporary queer cinema.

By returning to the hallmarks of his filmmaking approach, Araki was successfully able to remain faithful to his auteurist status while simultaneously avoiding the ever-enlarging "amoeba" of mainstream incorporation. The fact that his resulting creation ended up appealing to large numbers of alternative and mainstream audience members alike is a triumph for this auteur director. It is also a testament to the overall appeals of his distinctive cinematic vision, with its emphasis on alienation and consistent "outsider" point of view, when he remains faithful to it and employs it in relation to compelling (and queer) subject matter.

Afterword
Smiley Face and Beyond

From *Three Bewildered People in the Night* to *Mysterious Skin*, Araki's various films, like the cultural project of queer theory more generally, consistently challenged patriarchal hegemony's culturally influential notion that "only one sexuality (married-straight-white-man-on-top-of-woman-for-procreation-only) is normal and desirable" (Benshoff and Griffin 5-6) as well as what it means to be "normal," "(in)appropriate," or "deviant." Although the offerings he released in the late 1990s were not as groundbreaking as the ones that came before or after them, his cumulative body of work, through and including *Mysterious Skin*, nevertheless demonstrates that Araki consistently used the plasticity of the filmic medium, in new and unique ways, to explore the phenomenon of non-heterosexual lifestyles and sexual practices in the age of AIDS.

All of that changed considerably in 2007 with the release of Araki's ninth feature film, *Smiley Face*, a work that has nothing to do with non-heterosexual lifestyles or sexual practices in the age of AIDS whatsoever. Instead, it is a relatively stereotypical stoner comedy about an aspiring actress (with very limited aspirations) who experiences a daylong series of misadventures after she eats more than a dozen pot-laced cupcakes that she finds in the refrigerator she shares with her male roommate. Because *Smiley Face* is Araki's first film shot entirely from somebody else's screenplay, it represents a very different sort of offering than the other films analyzed at length as part of this project, all of which were written for the screen and directed by Araki himself and focused, at least in part, on either various forms of non-heterosexuality or at least atypical sexual and romantic relationships. As such, in-depth analysis of its contents and filmmaking approaches is not forthcoming here; however, a brief discussion of this film and its relation to Araki's prior works is provided.

Totally F***ed Up: *Smiley Face*

Smiley Face provides a day-in-the-life glimpse into the L.A. existence of Jane F. (played by Anna Faris), who, experiencing the munchies following her early morning bong hits, unwittingly becomes totally fucked up after she eats the aforementioned cupcakes that she discovers alongside a note from her roommate (played by Danny Masterson), who gives her the creeps, warning her not to consume them. As a result, over the course of the next several hours, she needs to purchase more pot to replace the brownies she ate, attend a late-morning acting audition, pay her apartment's electricity bill in person in order to keep the power on (or else suffer the repercussions of her roommate, whom she fears might be a skull-fucker), and repay her dope dealer (played by Adam Brody) the funds she owes him at the hemp festival taking place in Venice in order to stop him from stealing her furniture, including her beloved thousand-dollar bed. As can be expected, nothing goes smoothly for Jane in her attempts to accomplish these goals. Along the way, she inadvertently accepts a ride from a lovesick admirer, evades the police, makes off with an original copy of *The Communist Manifesto*, escapes in the back of a sausage truck, runs into both Carrot Top and Jesus, and finds herself stranded in midair on a Ferris wheel, all the while with her mouth hanging wide open. The overall contents of this film are perhaps best summed up in its review from *Cinema de Merde*:

> It's one-note and it's so far over the top, so obvious, that it all just sits there on the screen. [Jane] stares transfixed at a plastic volcano. She thinks things are taking longer than they are. She gets dry mouth. She gets the munchies. She brings up unrelated information in inappropriate settings. She gets paranoid. The best example of how not funny this movie is has Faris in a waiting room, reading a magazine upside-down. (par. 6)

Another critic similarly summarized the film's greatest flaw when he wrote, "Araki and screenwriter Dylan Haggerty beat a very simple premise—that this chick is baked out of her gourd—into the ground over and over again" (Antani, par. 2). Quite likely as a result, the film received extremely limited theatrical runs in Los Angeles and New York before being released quickly on DVD.

Although Araki admits that *Smiley Face* was a huge departure for him as a filmmaker, its screenplay by Haggerty possesses several noteworthy attributes that serve to explain why he would nevertheless find it to be an appealing project (D. Smith, par. 13). For starters, Jane's status as a hardcore pothead represents potentially controversial subject matter, at least for some audience members, as well as a variation on the theme of alternative lifestyles. In addition, throughout the film, Jane is presented as an outsider, a character type common in all of the director's films, who consistently makes poor decisions. The film's plot ultimately assumes the form of a road movie (similar to the plots of *The Living End* and *The Doom Generation*), as Jane must find a way to make it all the way from her nondescript L.A. neighborhood to Venice by her dealer's 3 p.m. deadline. The film's explicit incorporation of drug use makes it similar to Araki's storytelling approaches in *Totally F***ed Up, The Doom Generation, Nowhere*, and *Mysterious Skin*. By focusing primarily on the lived experiences of an aspiring L.A. actress, the film's approach is reminiscent of that of *Splendor*. The scene in which Brevin Ericson (played by John Krasinski) masturbates in the shower while fantasizing about Jane is reminiscent of the scene in *Nowhere* during which Dark masturbates in the shower while fantasizing about his girlfriend, his potential boyfriend, and the local dominatrix duo. As Jane devours Doritos in the home of her former professor, the loyal Araki fan very likely recalls the Doritos being consumed by Xavier during the closing scene of *The Doom Generation*. The film's overarching day-in-the-life format is certainly similar to Araki's approaches with *Totally F***ed Up* and *Nowhere*. Yet another substantial appeal of Haggerty's screenplay was that, after he made *Mysterious Skin*, which he regards as his most serious and darkest film to date, Araki wanted to do something entirely different and much lighter, and he recalled finding Haggerty's script to be hilarious when he read it years earlier; in fact, he regarded it as one of the funniest screenplays he had ever read (D'Arcy, par. 11; Kotek, par. 3; McKinley, par. 9). In numerous ways, therefore, it makes sense that Araki was attracted to Haggerty's screenplay, as it resonates with noteworthy aspects of his preceding cinematic offerings and allowed him to lighten up in terms of the subject matter of his next feature film.

At the same time, however, what is missing in *Smiley Face*, and what was so essential to all of his earlier works, is an emphasis on incorporating themes pertaining to non-heterosexuality, or at the very least atypical sexual and romantic relationships, which the director's fans had come to expect. Also missing in this film are the rawness, aggressive energy, disconcerting tone, and nihilistic themes common to Araki's preceding films, as well as many of the expected hallmarks of Araki's post-punk filmmaking style, including the incorporation of provocative images of non-heterosexual sexual activity and seemingly random acts of violence, defiance of cinematic convention, foregrounding of various human sexualities and sexual practices that have historically been marginalized by mainstream society, inclusion of bizarre street people and other marginal characters who populate a seemingly surrealistic Los Angeles, and an intentional lack of commercial appeal. Without these various attributes, the film ends up feeling as if it were made by an entirely different director, and its contents are quite disappointing to Araki's remaining loyal fans as a result.

Smiley Face is not a bad film per se. Anna Faris, for example, does a wonderful job of playing the hardcore stoner who is in every scene of this slapstick farce; her overall likeability keeps audience members rooting for her despite her character's numerous poor decisions, and her performance and comedic timing in this film have been likened to those of Buster Keaton, Carole Lombard, and Lucille Ball (D'Arcy, par. 13, 43; Lim, Halley, par. 9; Lim, par. 6). There are also a handful of truly humorous moments in the film, such as when Jane announces "I'm taking a shit!" and "Hold on—I'm shitting!" as she flushes pot down a public toilet, falsely believing that the cops are right on her tail, or when she appears to deliver an extremely eloquent Marxist rant while visiting a sausage factory, before the viewer is shown what Jane *actually* said in her extremely altered state. In fact, the offering is most noteworthy for Faris' skillful portrayal of non-normative (adult) femininity, which ultimately renders her character childlike and seemingly quite innocent despite all of the more vulgar aspects of her performance. Perhaps if Araki had put more of his own personal (and queer) touches on Haggerty's screenplay, rather than filming it primarily as Haggerty had written it, *Smiley Face* would feel more like a "Gregg Araki movie," and it would seem more worthy of extended analysis as yet another noteworthy expression of its director-(Araki)-as-auteur rather than, in this particular case, a noteworthy expression of its star-(Faris)-as-auteur. In its present incarnation, however, *Smiley Face* appears primarily to be yet another of Araki's failed, seemingly desperate attempts to attract larger, more mainstream audiences to view his various films. For as James Snyder noted in his *New York Sun* review of the film, "If this is meant as a lighthearted change of pace for Mr. Araki after *Mysterious Skin*, then perhaps he took things too far in the opposite direction. This isn't just light and fluffy; it floats away" (par. 1).

A Rocky Araki Future?

At the start of the third decade of his filmmaking career, Gregg Araki finds himself in a complex predicament. When he remains faithful to the original filmmaking goals and approaches that made him a leading figure of the New Queer Cinema, he ends up pleasing his loyal (and largely queer) audience and frequently ends up receiving substantial critical praise; however, the size of this audience is not substantial enough to deliver the sorts of profits that he needs to generate continual funding for future projects, and even the most generous critical praise does not typically end up paying the bills. When he deviates substantially from those filmmaking goals and approaches in an attempt to lure larger, more mainstream audiences to view his films, as he did most notably with *Splendor* and *Smiley Face*, he typically ends up alienating his core audience substantially while simultaneously failing to attract large numbers of new devotees. The question thus arises: What's a formerly boundary-pushing auteur director of the New Queer Cinema movement supposed to do?

At this particular historical moment, the future of Araki's filmmaking career remains murky and uncertain. When he rose to international cinematic prominence in the early 1990s, Araki self-identified (albeit somewhat reluctantly, as he does not appreciate simplistic and limiting categorization) as a queer filmmaker who makes queer films, and his earliest fans eagerly embraced him as such. Although, deep down, nobody really wants to restrict him to creating the same type of content time and time again, the expectation of this New Queer Cinema pioneer remains that he will continue to explore queer themes in his various offerings, despite the reality that the New Queer Cinema movement disintegrated more than a decade ago. The films that made Araki famous prominently featured the director's established in-your-face, post-punk authorial style, themes pertaining to non-heterosexual lifestyles and sexual practices in the age of AIDS, and extreme violent/sexual imagery, and they contained substantial radical/subversive potential as a result. At a minimum, therefore, Araki's remaining devoted fans expect these same attributes to be evident in the auteur director's various creations. When they are not, such as when he intentionally veers toward the mainstream, his resulting creations are widely regarded as being no longer particularly groundbreaking, culturally relevant, nor inherently interesting.

It has become clear in recent years that Araki feels somewhat trapped within his initial New Queer Cinema success. On the one hand, when asked in 2008 about the need to incorporate a queer sensibility in his various films, Araki stated, "I do think that definitely, for filmmakers like myself, Tom Kalin, Todd Haynes, Gus Van Sant, obviously the late Derek Jarman, our sexual identity definitely has a deep influence on our aesthetic and on the themes we deal with, and the kind of projects we're attracted to" (D. Smith, par. 17). On the other hand, when asked the same year about his filmmaking approaches and goals, Araki expressed, "As a filmmaker, I want to continually evolve and grow and challenge myself and do all kinds of different movies and work in a variety of genres—not just make the same film over and over again" (Halley, par. 21), and, when asked in 2009 about the New Queer Cinema label and its resulting expectations, Araki remarked, "Nobody ever attached that to Spike Lee. Oh, New Black Cinema! There's this weird need to categorize and put it in a box. I'm just interested in making movies that compel me" ("Outspoken," par. 19). During this latter interview, Araki also predicted that, two decades from now, both he and *Far From Heaven* director Todd Haynes will still be asked questions about the gay new wave, even if they are no longer making films pertaining to queer culture ("Outspoken," par. 18). Perhaps this is the burden that must be borne by an auteur director who, early in his filmmaking career, embraced the cachet of being a groundbreaking queer director at a particular historical moment when embodying such a status was trendy and cinematically welcomed. Perhaps this is a burden that is a bit too extreme and limiting for a director who self-identified as a gay man before becoming romantically involved with a woman for several years before pursuing romantic relationships with men once again.

As Araki stated in 1995, the year of *The Doom Generation*'s release, about the need for a new generation of innovative filmmakers who address contemporary concerns in original ways, "What The Movement (which, again, does not exist) really needs are those formal/political/thematic challengers of the Status Quo. . . . I'm talking about the next generation of Godards, Fassbinders, Derek Jarmans who push the envelope, who are not satisfied with the "Good Story Well Told" Bullshit that Mainstreams of all stripes and colors unabashedly endorse" (Moran 20). Given those noteworthy sentiments, it was quite disappointing to his fans when the auteur director went so extremely mainstream with *Splendor* before redeeming himself in their eyes with *Mysterious Skin*, especially because, early in his filmmaking career, Araki emphasized the "genuine need for the under- and misrepresented to identify themselves via the cinema machine" (qtd. in Moran 24). He disappointed them once again still further when he went even more mainstream with the release of *Smiley Face* in 2007.

With his various films from *Three Bewildered People in the Night* to *Mysterious Skin*, Araki, a self-proclaimed individual with a very strong personality who marches to the beat of his own drummer, established an especially intriguing (if not especially profitable) career breaking numerous cinematic taboos (D. Smith, par. 15; Halley, par. 26). About those works he has explained:

> I've always said that all my movies reflect many parts of my life, though none of them are straightforward autobiography. They express my worldview and serve as a Polaroid snapshot of where my head is at a particular time in my life. . . . Every film is three years out of my life and I will not be able to make that many while I'm on this planet, so it's not worth it for me to do anything I am not truly passionate about. . . . As a filmmaker, I just make the movie. People will interpret or misinterpret it however they see fit. That's the beauty of cinema: one person can see black, one can see white, and they can argue about it till the cows come home. (Hays, *View* 37, 39)

Accordingly, it is now up to all of his films' viewers—past, present, and future—to reflect on the contents of his various offerings—past, present, and (hopefully) future—and argue about them intelligently until those cattle arrive, which has been the primary objective of this particular project from its inception.

Supplementary Chapter
Cinematic Trash or Cultural Treasure? Conflicting Viewer Reactions to the Extremely Violent World of Bisexual Men in Gregg Araki's "Heterosexual Movie" *The Doom Generation*

The apparent status of Gregg Araki's *The Doom Generation* as cinematic trash was strongly suggested when critic Roger Ebert, reviewing the work in the *Chicago Sun-Times* shortly after its release in 1995, refused to award it any stars. In that review, Ebert dismissed the idea that the film contained any cultural value whatsoever by labeling it "the kind of movie where the film-maker hopes to shock you with sickening carnage and violent amorality, while at the same time holding himself carefully aloof from it with his style" (par. 1). He continued:

This is a road picture about Amy and Jordan, young druggies who get in-volved with a [bisexual] drifter named Xavier who challenges their ideas about sex, both gay and straight, while involving them on a blood-soaked cross-country odyssey. The movie opens as the drifter "inadvertently" (Araki's word, in the press kit) blows off the head of a Korean convenience store owner. The head lands in the hotdog relish and keeps right on screaming. Ho, ho. . . . Wait, there's more: "As the youthful band of out-siders continues their travels through the wasteland of America, Amy finds herself [having sex with] both Jordan and Xavier, forging a triangle of love, sex, and desperation too pure for this world. . . ." Further reading from the [press] kit: "*The Doom Generation* is the Alienated Teen Pic to

91

End All Alienated Teen Pics—and, oh yeah, it's a comedy and a love story,
too." Oh, yeah. (Ebert, par. 4, 9)

Since then, countless additional film critics have agreed with Ebert's assessment. For example, writing in *Film Comment*, Gavin Smith observed
that, with *The Doom Generation*, "Araki goes gross-out with a vengeance:
the film is a gleeful panic of severed heads, spurting arteries, rape, and cas-
tration" ("Sundance 'Kids'" 9). In his *Entertainment Weekly* review, Steve
Daly wrote, "For those who haven't walked out before the closing credits,
good luck searching for meaning—you'll find mostly blood and epithets"
(40). The online critics who refer to themselves collectively as the Mutant
Reviewers From Hell have concluded, in a series of individual reviews, that
"*[The] Doom Generation* is just a piece of trash, and there is no debate about
it—none" (Justin, par. 4); "The socially redeeming value is in the negative
numbers" (PoolMan, par. 5); "This film hurts you. It ruined my day when I
rented it, just because it did succeed in catching the events in depressing
lives of people scraped from the bottom of the scum barrel. Gross people
doing gross things, conceived by people who should have never made a film
in the first place" (Kyle, par. 2); and "This movie is a cinematic masterpiece—master piece of CRAP!" (Clare, par. 1). But are all of these critics,
and so many others like them, actually missing the entire point of the film?

I have long maintained that *The Doom Generation* is a cultural treasure,
rather than a piece of cinematic trash. In fact, I find it to be such a powerful
and culturally significant film that I have exposed students to it in the various film courses I have taught, at three colleges and universities, from the
year of its release to the present. As I have argued elsewhere (Hart, "Auteur"
30-38), in my view, by placing three young people on the road after they
unwittingly commit a series of murders, Araki creates a utopic setting in this
film within which two attractive young men, Xavier Red (played by Johnathon Schaech) and Jordan White (played by James Duval), can explore their
growing mutual sexual attraction and most intimate sexual desires. At the
same time, while they are both becoming more comfortable with the idea of
sleeping together, they both repeatedly sleep with Jordan's girlfriend, Amy
Blue (played by Rose McGowan), until the three end up having sex together.
Unfortunately, just before Xavier and Jordan are about to consummate their
sexual relationship without Amy being present, an especially brutal climax
prevents that act from occurring: a trio of gaybashing neo-Nazi thugs—who
in an earlier scene perceived Xavier's non-heterosexual "otherness" when
they encountered him in a record store, commented on his "pretty earrings"
and "hot, tight bubble butt," and referred to him as a "shy, sensitive
flower"—discover Xavier and Jordan naked and alone in bed together, conclude that the "world'll be a purer place" when the "two little faggots" are

both dead, and proceed to chop off Jordan's "puny, worthless cock" using gardening shears; he dies almost immediately. Although this unexpected, remarkably brutal bloodbath at the film's end leaves many viewers in a mild state of shock when they initially encounter it, I have always felt that it effectively represents Araki's way of making an incredibly powerful statement about the repressive nature of hegemonic ideology in the United States in relation to bisexual men and other non-heterosexual individuals. As such, I have continually maintained that this film contains substantial cultural value, even though it may not seem to on its surface.

Occasionally, I stumble upon an analysis of *The Doom Generation* that agrees with my perspective. For example, writing in *Film Quarterly*, James Moran noted, "For despite the polish of its imagery and its apparent focus upon straight sexuality, *The Doom Generation*, in both its form and its content, continued to develop Araki's unique aesthetic vision and critical gay voice, which together bind each of his films into a unified body of work" (18-19). In addition, film critic Robin Wood concluded that "No film more precisely captures my own sense of where we are and where we are going" (336). The clear majority of reviews and analyses of this film that I have read to date, however, condemn this cinematic offering as pointless rubbish. In part, this may be because Araki—such as by giving his characters in this work the last names of Red, White, and Blue, something noted by several critics but never adequately elaborated upon thereafter—appears to be dealing with his subject matter in over-the-top and seemingly superficial ways (whether or not this is actually the case), in a manner that is immediately off-putting to the majority of popular critics. Such sentiments likely led an *Entertainment Weekly* critic to state, "Not for everyone, the film should give fans of *Natural Born Killers* an even more rewarding demonstration of the aesthetics of willful incoherence" (Kenny 68), or an *Artforum* critic to conclude, "Araki's script fills characters' mouths with ridiculously tweaked youthspeak . . . at once too clever to seem spontaneous and too lame to signify anything but authorial condescension toward his unlikable protagonists" (Cooper 22).

As a result of these various observations and reviews, I have begun in recent years to wonder whether I am forcing my own analysis on the film, rather than identifying cultural meaning that is viably contained in, and/or produced through viewing, the film itself. To explore this issue, I recently asked a group of undergraduate students, enrolled in an upper-division film and television studies course at a small liberal arts college, to view *The Doom Generation* during the first class meeting of a new semester (as I have done regularly on the first day of this particular course each semester) and to document their reactions (positive and/or negative) to it in written form, working individually and without access to any textual or online materials about the film that have been written by others. Upon their completion of that task, I invited these students, on a voluntary basis and with informed consent, to authorize me (in writing) to analyze, summarize, and directly quote their written reactions to the film, anonymously, in this essay. The students were assured that their decision of whether or not to provide such authorization would have no impact whatsoever on their course grades or my perceptions of them as students, and they were informed that any authorized responses would be identified only by gender (rather than first name, etc.) in any research essay I ultimately composed. All fifteen students (eight males and seven females) enrolled in the course opted to participate in this study.

This process differed somewhat from the way that I usually introduce students to Araki's film. I screen the film the same way each semester during our first class meeting, but then I typically ask students to offer their reactions (positive and/or negative) in verbal, rather than written, form as part of an entire-group discussion. I next lead the students, using the various points they raised as well as my personal insights, in a thorough analysis of the film's contents to show how all of the various elements of *The Doom Generation* (i.e., plot, dialogue, lighting, symbolism, elements of mise-en-scène, etc.) can be perceived as potentially adding up to a coherent and compelling statement about American ideology in relation to bisexual men and other non-heterosexual individuals, in order to demonstrate the various ways that viewers can make meaning from a cinematic text. This time around, however, the students were asked to provide and submit their individual reactions to the film in written form first, so that they would not be influenced by the views and opinions of their peers, before an entire-group discussion and analysis of the film occurred. Furthermore, I did not share any of my own impressions of the film with the students until after all written reactions had formally been submitted for analysis. What follows is a summary of what I learned from this process.

The Distinction Between Message and Meaning

Cultural studies scholarship over the past three decades has continuously revealed that there is a vast difference between the "message" that a filmmaker or other media professional intends to communicate with a specific media offering and the actual "meaning" that is derived by audience members as they encounter that same offering. In other words, the distinction between "message" and "meaning" in relation to a media offering is quite significant because, whereas the manifest content of a media message (in print, sounds, visuals, etc.) can be observed directly and potentially identically by all of its audience members and is largely "fixed," the range of viable meanings derived from identical media content by different individuals is variable, not entirely self-evident, and relatively "unfixed" (McQuail 304).

Whereas early mass communication theorists conceptualized the process of communication in terms of a top-down, linear model of message dissemination proceeding quite efficiently from sender to receiver—in which a message created by a sender gets interpreted by all of its receivers precisely as the sender intended—cultural studies scholars have consistently maintained and demonstrated that there are noteworthy differences in the ways that media messages are actually "read" (or "decoded") by the individuals who receive them, despite the sender's original intentions. With his influential essay "Encoding/Decoding," for example, Stuart Hall was among the first cultural studies scholars to introduce the idea that various forms of media content do not contain a single meaning that is decoded efficiently by all receivers, but rather are typically read in somewhat different ways by different individuals (or even by the same individuals in different contexts or at different times in their lives). Hall argues that, rather than interpreting a media message precisely as it was intended by its sender, or reacting to a media message in exactly the opposite way as the sender would expect, most receivers regularly decode media messages in the form of a "negotiated reading," which means they perceive and/or accept some aspects of the message as the sender intended, and they simultaneously overlook and/or reject other aspects of that same message (136-38). In the field of literary studies, this phenomenon has been referred to as representing the "death of the author," in recognition of the reality that the ultimate creation of any "author" (or sender of a media offering) does not contain only a single "message" or "meaning" that may be communicated to and derived by audience members but is, rather, multi-dimensional; as such, the "reader" (or receiver) of that media offering actually determines the "meaning" of the work by reacting to the various dimensions of its contents in relation to his or her own biography, history, psychology, and previous interactions with a wide range of related media offerings, despite what the author may have initially intended (Barthes 146, 148).

In relation to gay men, lesbians, bisexuals, and transgenders, these noteworthy theoretical concepts have been expanded upon in recent years to demonstrate how possessing a non-heterosexual social identity represents, in the words of Brett Farmer, a "difference that makes a difference" (6), one that frequently results in different ways of "seeing" and "decoding" media offerings than heterosexual individuals typically utilize. In part, such decoding differences stem frequently from "strategies that reveal subtexts and subversive readings in a more complex system than the patriarchal heterosexual system assumes" (Straayer 2); in addition, they often result from the various character behaviors, contradictions, gestures, images, narrative am-

biguities, subplots, themes, and related attributes of a film or other media offering that non-heterosexual audience members choose to foreground during
the viewing experience, ones that the majority of "heterosexual audience
members tend to overlook or repress, either because they are oblivious to
them or frightened by them" (Hart, "Gay" 3). Such differences are effective
at explaining how, historically, non-heterosexual audience members have
derived unique types of viewing pleasure from Hollywood films and other
media offerings that exclusively feature overtly heterosexual narratives and
characters, as well as how they may derive unique sorts of meanings (as
compared to those derived by heterosexual audience members) from viewing
films explicitly featuring gay, lesbian, bisexual, and transgender narratives,
themes, and characters today. At the same time, as cultural studies scholars
Caroline Evans and Lorraine Gamman have so insightfully pointed out, the
type of individuals one chooses to sleep with (with regard to his or her sexual orientation) does not absolutely determine how one decodes media messages (40).

As such, it is important to note that, as with all other types of individuals
who possess a range of important demographic characteristics (in terms of
race, class, gender, sexual orientation, etc.), and in accordance with the
findings of cultural studies theorists, it certainly cannot be assumed that all
non-heterosexual audience members who view the same film or other media
offering will necessarily decode the work in similar ways; instead, because
they (like all other types of viewers) will naturally foreground different aspects of the work during the viewing experience, their decodings of the
work's contents will typically contain noteworthy variations. This important
reality helps to explain why the majority of heterosexual audience members,
as well as many non-heterosexual audience members, who view a film such
as *From Here to Eternity* (Fred Zinnemann, 1953) do not detect that it contains a substantial bisexual subtext pertaining to a love story between War-
den (played by Burt Lancaster), a man's man who is respected both by his
superiors and the G.I.'s he leads, and Pvt. Robert E. Lee Prewitt (played by
Montgomery Clift), a skilled bugler and former boxer, both of whom simultaneously pursue romantic and sexual relationships with women to some degree over the course of its narrative, or that, rather than offering a straightforward narrative about a heterosexual FBI agent (played by Keanu Reeves)
who seeks a romantic relationship with an attractive female surfer (played by
Lori Petty), the film *Point Break* (Kathryn Bigelow, 1991) may actually be
primarily about the agent's bisexual attraction to and relationship with the
woman's former boyfriend (played by Patrick Swayze), the leader of the
bank robbers in the film, instead (Hart, "Gay" 16). The goal of the present
study pertaining to *The Doom Generation*, therefore, was to determine what
sorts of noteworthy meanings (if any) are produced by various individuals

through the experience of viewing the film, a complex work exploring bi-sexuality and bisexual desires that was intentionally promoted (as well as identified during the work's opening title sequence) as "a heterosexual movie by Gregg Araki" in order to appeal to a wider range of audience members than the director's earlier New Queer Cinema offerings (such as 1992's *The Living End* and 1993's *Totally F***ed Up*).

The Doom Generation as Cinematic Trash

As previously stated, *The Doom Generation* features the road-trip (mis)adventures of three rootless young people who, in the wake of mur-dering a Korean Quickie Mart owner and others, push the boundaries of sex-ual pleasure and experimentation: Xavier, an attractive, bisexual drifter; Jor-dan, a dim and seemingly innocent teen; and Amy, Jordan's caustic, drug-using girlfriend and Xavier's occasional sex partner. With this film, Araki has effectively created a "road movie in which the characters never actually seem to go anywhere" (Kenny 68); as such, the film shares with its contents feelings of boredom, futility, and pointlessness. The most attention-grabbing narrative developments feature Xavier having increasingly kinky sex with Amy in order to entice Jordan into bed with him—resulting in numerous sex scenes that border on the pornographic—as well as extreme instances of vis-ceral violence that leave a severed head talking in a pool of relish and on-ions, a severed arm spurting blood all over a car's interior, and Jordan's sev-ered penis being inserted into Xavier's mouth by their group of assailants during the film's climax.

It is perhaps unsurprising, therefore, that all fifteen students who viewed and wrote about their reactions to *The Doom Generation* identified a range of potentially harmful elements in the film. One student was concerned about the abrasive dialogue in the film—including lines spoken by Amy such as "Eat my fuck" and "Kindly pull your head out of your rectal re-gion"—and felt the film had no plot aside from presenting the main charac-ters' ongoing experimentations with sex, drugs, and murder. Another felt that the graphic penis-chopping scene during the film's climax might lead many viewers to regard such violence as justified when it is directed toward bisexual men or other non-heterosexual individuals. Others were concerned that the lack of consequences for the trio's acts of violence, as well as the lack of remorse they felt after committing them, might lead to real-life in-stances of copycat crimes (one student even referred to the April 1999 shootings at Colorado's Columbine High School in this regard), or that the developments in the film would lead some young viewers to conclude that people in American society can no longer live together in harmony, potentially resulting in the self-fulfilling prophecy that already-violent conditions in U.S. society will only continue to worsen over time.

Several students offered generalized assessments of the film that revealed they regarded it to be cinematic trash, pure and simple. For example, one female student stated, "*The Doom Generation* is an aspect of life I disagree with. . . . The film left me feeling angry [and] disturbed. . . . I could only imagine the images that would run through my dreams at night." Echoing such sentiments in greater depth, a male student explained, "After watching *The Doom Generation*, I was certainly shocked. I can honestly say that I hated the movie [from start] to [finish]. It's a disgusting, immoral, unnecessary movie filled with content that does not need to be shown in a film. . . . All around, this movie sets as bad of an example as you can. . . . I personally don't understand why this movie was made."

Most students articulated their concerns with regard to specific aspects of the film. Several were concerned about the effects that viewing the uncontrolled lifestyle of these three rootless young people might have on the film's audience members. A male student wrote, "The movie shows its main characters doing drugs, smoking cigarettes, drinking beer, eating junk food, and, of course, killing the people that were trying to kill them. All of these things are bad for you and could cause social chaos." Similarly, a female student cautioned, "This movie contradicts everything that a parent would probably say. These reckless teens had no curfews, no rules, and no limits. If every young person were like that, our society would be chaotic."

The unconventional sexual situations portrayed in *The Doom Generation* also generated criticism. As one male student stated, "Both X [as Xavier is often referred to in the film] and Jordan masturbate while watching the other engage in sexual activity; it seems to bother neither. Parents might be shocked to find voyeurism and autoeroticism displayed so bluntly. When thrown into the mix of other sexual themes, this is probably the least of their concerns." Another male student elaborated on such concerns:

> Amy and Jordan are a couple, and they say that they are in love with each other. They seem to be a healthy pair until Amy goes behind Jordan's back and sleeps with Xavier. Personally, I don't like cheating, I don't cheat myself, and I look down on it very much. I believe that this is a common viewpoint [held] by many other people, as well. This scene made me feel bad for Jordan, as well as a little sick; it was only the beginning of that, though. The next time that Amy and Xavier slept together, Jordan watched from outside the hotel window. More and more casual sexual behavior kept going throughout the movie, until the end where all three of them were [in bed] together. That lifestyle seemed unhealthy and awkward to me; I certainly can't appreciate it. I couldn't understand why Jordan seemed okay with it, either.

To varying degrees, all fifteen students who viewed and shared their re-actions to *The Doom Generation* felt that it contained negative, potentially harmful attributes of various kinds. Their comments clearly pertain to the concept of dystopian fears associated with cinematic reception, which regard exposure to film images as a potentially evil force that might ultimately pro-duce social chaos or, at the very least, a range of negative social effects. A primary concern historically in this regard, as relevant to the contents of *The Doom Generation*, is that cinematic images might ultimately encourage viewers to indulge regularly in "curiositas," which involves the attraction to unbeautiful, extreme, or even morbid sights simply to satisfy one's curiosity or "lust of the eyes" (Gunning 871). Does this mean, therefore, that the stu-dents' responses confirmed that *The Doom Generation* is undeniably a prime example of cinematic trash? Not necessarily.

The Doom Generation as Cultural Treasure

Like the majority of film critics who have written about *The Doom Genera-tion* to date, there are many individuals who are unable to find any socially redeeming value in this cinematic offering. For example, one female student who visited my campus office nearly a week after viewing Araki's film ex-plained that, after devoting several days to considering what good could pos-sibly come from making or viewing such a film, she stood firm in her initial belief that nothing positive could ever come from it.

Despite that conclusion, seven of the fifteen students (four males and three females) who shared their reactions to *The Doom Generation* in this study were indeed able to find significant degrees of cultural value in the film, even if they simultaneously held some concerns about its contents. As one male student accurately pointed out, "The way the film is interpreted will vary from person to person. More pleasure will be derived from those who accept the film as art. . . . It is important to remember that there is a second side to every story. Films like [*The Doom Generation*] can bring about social change by those intellectuals (both young and old) who see be-yond Rose McGowan's bare breasts and see a generation of youth crying out for help." I couldn't have said it better myself.

One female student viewed *The Doom Generation* as a cautionary tale, warning about the need to intervene in the lives of modern young people and ensure that they feel valued and loved. She wrote:

> I see the movie being positive in showing how people in our society—even young, innocent people—can turn out, all starting with a sense of not be-longing. In the beginning of the movie, Amy said [to Jordan], "There's no

place for us in this world." Just that comment says a lot about what the movie is trying to [say]. They don't fit in. The movie was an extreme way of showing what those feelings of being "different" can lead to. . . . It subtly goes deep into how and why people would live this way. If you can't see the inside of a life like that, it is easy to judge. It is really easy for society to look at people like Amy, Jordan, and Xavier and look down upon them, rather than finding out what went wrong, and what could have been done to avoid it. . . . I think it would be easy for somebody to just look at this film negatively, but I don't think that the filmmaker wanted that. I don't think that he is some deranged person; I think he had a great point.

Other students felt that the extreme acts of violence in the film were not really a cause for concern. As a male student explained:

The three main characters in *The Doom Generation* represent three different stereotypical personalities in society. Amy is a headstrong, dirty-mouthed, self-[absorbed], individualistic girl who becomes the sex slave [of] the other two characters. Jordan, Amy's boyfriend, is a passive, non-aggressive, dependent type who is not phased by the fact that his girlfriend is sleeping with some guy they picked up on the road. Xavier—or as he is referred to in the movie, X—is an aggressive, sadistic, controlling, heartless murderer who was picked up by Amy and Jordan at the beginning of the movie. The personalities were too extreme to be taken seriously. . . . It is obvious [from] watching these characters that they are very unrealistic and that the acts they participated in would not be reenacted by most level-headed members of society. . . .

The director made a point of producing each violent sequence so over-the-top that it was humorous. A key reason for creating such scenes is to attack society's preconceived ideas of teenagers and what they do. The film makes a point of showing such extreme characters that they mock the members of society who think that teenagers are a source of chaos in themselves. . . . It's basically showing lots of negative things but then saying, "Hey, relax, don't take this so seriously—it's entertainment."

The majority of students who identified cultural value in the film, however, tended to point out that *The Doom Generation* can, ultimately, bring about positive social change in U.S. society because it addresses and attacks the concept of discrimination in relation to bisexuals and others. For example, a male student stated:

The theme of evil is demonstrated throughout the film from the "666" plastered on all the [cash] registers to the signs on the motels and stores proclaiming [that] the end is near. In this movie, these characters are seen as evil mainly because they are different. After the first murder is committed by Xavier, the news broadcast states that the earring found at the murder scene belonged to a Satanist, homosexual, or punk kid, implying that all of [them] are evil because they are different. . . . By watching this film, I think the audience will see that everyone is unique in their own way and that [just] because someone is different it doesn't mean they are evil. . . . In the case of this film, it isn't just displaying how to murder, abuse drugs, and have sex. It is giving us something to think about regarding today's society and the feeling of alienation.

Expanding upon such notions, another male student noted:

It has opened a door for people that are either gay or bisexual or even interested in the gothic style of clothing. . . . Throughout the film, we see things that society has told us are bad. . . . As the film goes on, we see Amy and X have sex, we see Jordan masturbate as X and Amy have sex, and we even see the three characters have a threesome. These things could be bad for society, but isn't that just what society says? Who says it is bad to have a threesome? Do we not live in a society that believes in individual freedom of expression and, for the most part, in a society where sex is not a taboo?

One of the strongest points made was at the end of the film, when, [as Xavier and Jordan are alone in bed together, three] of the guys who thought they knew Amy earlier in the film rape her on an American flag and cut Jordan's penis off. I thought this was a strong point for Araki because I believe he was trying to say that there are worse people out in this world than Amy, X, and Jordan. He had the flag and the national anthem playing, I think, to show what idiots racist people [are] and how uneducated they are. The movie works in a unique way of trying to tell the viewers of it not to pick on people different from yourself because you are afraid of the unknown, and I think that is a great social benefactor. . . . I let the film sink in and realized that all Araki was trying to do was to say we should not judge people so quickly, and it is okay to be who we are. In that aspect, I think it sends a [positive] message.

Similarly, a female student explained that discriminatory views end up being reduced by the film's end as a result of viewers' vicarious participation in the lives of the film's three main characters:

Throughout the film, the audience experiences [a] life different from their own, which causes some viewers [to] question their own values and beliefs. . . . There were several times when I looked away, covering my eyes and ears, but that did not stop me from wanting to watch more. I wanted to explore the rest of the movie; I was curious about what was going to happen. . . . I asked myself, "Were Xavier and Jordan going to have sexual relations?" "Why would anyone have Jesus tattooed on [his] penis?"

I was so involved in the film that these controversial images did not bother me. This is how this film brings about change for social good. I am a heterosexual female [who is] not exactly comfortable with even watching men and women have sex, let alone two men or two women, but during this film it did not matter. I was able to explore a world that was so different from my own. I accepted what was going on throughout the film because I wanted to see more. The power that this film had was so great because it allowed the viewer to put down their conscience and explore new concepts that are usually unmentionable. . . . We experience different lifestyles in movies that allow the viewers to possibly change their opinion on homosexuality or men being closer than just friends.

Finally, another female student captured the essence of all of these preceding arguments when she so articulately concluded:

> The utopian feeling that I received from watching this film was about how, after a certain amount of time, the three teenagers were able to accept [bisexuality] within a group, together. Xavier was already open to having sex with both males and females and brought forth new ideas into Amy's and Jordan's minds. Amy was a little hesitant about the idea at the beginning, and Jordan had never experienced anything like it, [but] soon they grew to accept the idea. Xavier brought many new ideas into this couple's minds and opened their eyes to a different meaning of existence. At the beginning of the movie, Amy only thought about death and how "there was no place in the world" for them; as the film progressed, it helped to show that there was a meaning to life and ways of being happy. . . .
>   This film truly opened my eyes to the way our American culture really is. We think we are such a free country, but when you really think about it, we are one of the most hypocritical countries out there. We say we have freedom of speech, but when you speak the words [that] people don't want to hear, somebody always has something critical to say and harasses you about decisions that you make in life. It is difficult to be accepted in our country unless you are "normal" and try to be the "perfect" person but, in reality, who is perfect? Whose right is it to say [that] what you do is right or wrong?

After reading all of these additional reactions to *The Doom Generation*, I was impressed with the insights and conviction they contained, especially upon acknowledging that most of these students were discussing a film that they did not particularly like nor enjoy in the first place.

Concluding Observations

Until relatively recently, Hollywood's powers-that-be have long regarded topics such as adultery and impotence as providing perfectly acceptable cinematic fare, whereas bisexuality and other forms of non-heterosexuality have been their *bête noire* (Custen 128). When bisexuality did appear on film, it was typically used to "disguise or legitimize homosexuality" because bisexuality itself has historically been viewed as being "freaky," and bisexual characters have been disparaged for being "half faggot" (Russo 230-31). Accordingly, as activist Wayne Bryant explains in the preface to his book *Bisexual Characters in Film: From Anaïs to Zee*:

> Anyone with a passing interest in the subject can probably name a dozen or more movies with gay and lesbian characters. The same is not true for bisexual characters in film. Experts may be hard-pressed to cite more than two or three examples, even though many films with homosexuality as a central theme have bisexual protagonists. The invisibility of bisexual characters in film is compounded by the dearth of writing on the topic. (ix)

Both Gregg Araki's film *The Doom Generation*, as well as this essay, are intended to begin to rectify this quite problematic state of affairs.

The defiant, subversive essence of the various films created as part of the New Queer Cinema phenomenon of the 1990s was directed both toward mainstream homophobic individuals in U.S. society and the "tasteful and tolerated" non-heterosexuals who cohabit with them virtually invisibly (Aaron 7). A primary goal of New Queer Cinema filmmakers (including Araki) was to give voice to marginalized members of the LGBT community, as well as to members of its various subgroups (e.g., black gay men, Hispanic bisexual women, etc.), in order to enlighten all people about the realities of forging a non-heterosexual existence in a heterocentric—and frequently blatantly homophobic—world (Aaron 3-4). As such, it is perhaps unsurprising that common themes in Araki's various films (including *The Doom Generation*) involve alienation, betrayal, detachment, emptiness, and "a present that's really fucked up" (Chang 49), or that typical scenarios in them involve intense romantic and sexual pairings between gay and bisexual men as well as complex love triangles involving two (bisexual or heterosexual) men and a (bisexual or heterosexual) woman (Hart, "Auteur" 35). It is perhaps further unsurprising that, during the decade of the 1990s, Araki succeeded in substantially reworking several popular Hollywood subgenres (e.g., buddy films, juvenile delinquency films, and road movies) into non-heterosexual variations, using his directorial "gay sensibility" to present even apparently "straight material" in homoerotic ways, such as by eroticizing attractive male torsos (by forcing the camera to linger on them and shoot them from low angles) or by focusing intentionally on extended, intense eye contact between two sexually charged, breathtaking young men (Chang 50; Grundmann 25; Moran 19). Openly acknowledging this reality, Araki himself has called *The Doom Generation* "the gayest 'heterosexual movie' ever made" (G. Smith, "Sundance 'Kids'" 9).

When I first began incorporating *The Doom Generation* in the various film courses I teach, more than a decade ago, I did so enthusiastically because I realized that, upon conclusion of the initial viewing experience, most viewers are tempted to dismiss it immediately as cinematic trash. In fact, that was even my own immediate reaction to the film when I first experienced it. I recognized that it would be difficult for many of my students—who typically have been raised on a steady diet of mainstream Hollywood movies from an early age—to decide what to make of this complex and challenging work, but that is what has been so fun about exposing them to this film all of these years. In my experience to date, far too many viewers wish to instantly dismiss *The Doom Generation* and other of Araki's films as the kinds of offerings "jeered at not only just by critics, but also by drunken teenagers, prison inmates, and medicated zoo animals" (qtd. in Hershenson, par. 9), as critic Jason Katzman has done, rather than to wrestle with their complex and challenging contents in the more intellectually informed and enlightened ways they appear to require.

It is perhaps especially noteworthy, therefore, that so few of the students who participated in this study made note of the various ways that *The Doom Generation* can be regarded as an "art film," rather than simply a film containing political themes and messages. In my earlier essay "Auteur/Bricoleur/Provocateur: Gregg Araki and Post-punk Style in *The Doom Generation*," I demonstrate at length how this director's post-punk filmmaking style contributes substantially, at the intersection of the artistic and the political, to this film's radical/subversive potential with regard to cinematic representations and social constructions of bisexual men and other non-heterosexual individuals (30-38). What many of the critics who immediately dismiss *The Doom Generation* as cinematic trash appear to overlook is that Araki, as a graduate of the University of Southern California's School of Cinema-Television, is well familiar with film history and theory and various influential works of cinematic auteurs from previous decades, including those of Jean-Luc Godard, who has had a substantial influence on Araki's own creations. For example:

> Araki regularly incorporates the disjointed narrative techniques (jumpcuts, handheld cameras, nonlinearity, etc.) of Godard's films, and he agrees with Godard that outsiders can indeed reject traditional conceptions of film realism yet still work within the cinema industry in order to change it. If a key component of a post-punk style is bricolage, Araki functions as bricoleur in the way that he modifies Godard's techniques in order to produce films of even greater subversive potential. His post-punk bricolage is seen even more clearly in the way he plays with the conventions of various genres in order to make them serve new and radical purposes. (Hart, "Auteur" 32-33)

Despite the aesthetic complexity of Araki's film, I suspect that it is this director's embracing and foregrounding of a "schizophrenic" visual style—one that is based on the "fragmentation of time into a series of perpetual presents" (Jameson 125)—that causes many viewers and critics to tend to overlook its noteworthy artistic attributes which, on the surface, appear primarily to offer a "seemingly disconnected, discontinuous stringing together of narrative images that [seem to] fail to offer a coherent global meaning" (Hart, "Auteur" 34), rather than to pack an even more powerful representational and political punch. As a result, viewers who perceive this film to be "trash" rather than "art" most likely let their guard down substantially while viewing it, thereby potentially leaving them more vulnerable to being influenced by its politically charged messages, themes, and representations than they otherwise might be because they are far less likely to reflect thoughtfully upon, and/or argue actively against, them during the viewing experience.

It has long been said that one person's (cinematic) trash is another person's (cultural) treasure. This appears to hold true with regard to Gregg Araki's 1995 film, *The Doom Generation*. As the responses documented in this study show, approximately half of the students who viewed this film derived meanings from it that offered them new insights into the conditions experienced regularly by bisexual men and other non-heterosexual individuals in modern U.S. society, including various forms of discrimination and recurring feelings of otherness and alienation that derive from constantly being judged by conservative hegemonic social standards. When all was said and done, the results of this research project convinced me that cultural value lies in the eye of the beholder and that there is indeed a great deal of cultural value that can be derived from viewing this intriguing film, even if the majority of its viewers fail—or perhaps simply refuse—to recognize it. Paradoxically speaking, even cinematic works that appear on their surface to be trash can contain substantial cultural value as they lead their viewers to stretch beyond their comfort zones and vicariously experience circumstances, events, and lifestyles to which they are not especially accustomed.

Like punk musical offerings in their heyday, *The Doom Generation* and other of Araki's films are readily recognizable by their intentionally raw depictions of extreme aggression, angst, nihilism, and sexuality that lack conventional commercial appeal, in narratives pertaining to dysfunctional young people striving desperately to forge any sort of meaningful relationship with another. In my opinion, those attributes are what make them so intriguing, as well as so culturally threatening to many. In short, Araki's various films vividly and powerfully embody the very undercurrents of anarchy, disorder, and (sexual) otherness that civilized societies of all kinds have, for generations, been striving to repress at virtually any cost, yet which nevertheless may be quite necessary in order to further the progress that remains to be made toward the acceptance of bisexuality and other non-heterosexual identities today (Arnold 11).

Summarizing his reactions to *The Doom Generation*, one of my students stated, "The movie takes everything that critics would hate about a movie and brings them out for the viewer. To me, that [represents] Araki, in essence, giving the critics the middle finger and making the film that he wanted to." I suspect that was Araki's intention—and main point—all along.

Filmography

1987
Three Bewildered People in the Night
Cinematography: Gregg Araki. Director: Gregg Araki. Film Editing: Gregg Araki. Producer: Gregg Araki. Screenwriter: Gregg Araki. U.S. Release Date: Did not receive widespread distribution. With Mark Howell (David), John Lacques (Craig), Darcy Marta (Alicia). Currently unavailable on DVD.

1989
The Long Weekend (O' Despair)
Cinematography: Gregg Araki. Director: Gregg Araki. Film Editing: Gregg Araki. Producer: Gregg Araki. Screenwriter: Gregg Araki. U.S. Release Date: May 17, 1991 (limited). With Andrea Beane (Leah), Marcus D'Amico (Greg), Nicole Dillenberg (Sara), Maureen Dondanville (Rachel), Bretton Vail (Michael), Lance Woods (Alex). Currently unavailable on DVD.

1992
The Living End
Cinematography: Gregg Araki. Director: Gregg Araki. Film Editing: Gregg Araki. Producers: Jon Gerrans, Marcus Hu. Screenwriter: Gregg Araki. U.S. Release Date: August 21, 1992. With Mike Dytri (Luke), Craig Gilmore (Jon), Darcy Marta (Darcy), Scot Goetz (Peter), Johanna Went (Fern), Mary Woronov (Daisy), Christopher Mabli (NeoNazi). Currently available on DVD from Strand Releasing.

1993
*Totally F***ed Up*

Cinematography: Gregg Araki. Director: Gregg Araki. Film Editing: Gregg Araki. Producers: Gregg Araki, Andrea Sperling. Screenwriter: Gregg Araki. U.S. Release Date: October 10, 1993. With James Duval (Andy), Susan Behshid (Michele), Roko Belic (Tommy), Jenee Gill (Patricia), Gilbert Luna (Steven), Lance May (Deric), Alan Boyce (Ian). Currently available on DVD from Strand Releasing.

1995
The Doom Generation

Cinematography: Jim Fealy. Director: Gregg Araki. Film Editing: Gregg Araki, Jennifer Gentile, Karen Kennedy, Kate McGowan. Producers: Gregg Araki, Yves Marmion, Andrea Sperling. Screenwriter: Gregg Araki. U.S. Release Date: October 27, 1995. With Johnathon Schaech (Xavier Red), James Duval (Jordan White), Rose McGowan (Amy Blue), Dustin Nguyen (Quickiemart Clerk), Margaret Cho (Clerk's Wife), Christopher Knight (TV Anchorman), Lauren Tewes (TV Anchorwoman), Parker Posey (Brandi). Currently available on DVD from Lions Gate Home Entertainment.

1997
Nowhere

Cinematography: Arturo Smith. Director: Gregg Araki. Film Editing: Gregg Araki, Jennifer Gentile, Jeff Malmberg, Anthony Santiago. Producers: Gregg Araki, Andrea Sperling. Screenwriter: Gregg Araki. U.S. Release Date: May 9, 1997. With James Duval (Dark), Nathan Bexton (Montgomery), Rachel True (Mel), Kathleen Robertson (Lucifer), Alan Boyce (Handjob), Chiara Mastroianni (Kriss), Debi Mazar (Kozy), Jeremy Jordan (Bart), Guillermo Diaz (Cowboy), Jordan Ladd (Alyssa), Christina Applegate (Dingbat), Sarah Lassez (Egg/Polly), Jaason Simmons (The Teen Idol), Ryan Phillippe (Shad), Heather Graham (Lilith), Scott Caan (Ducky), Thyme Lewis (Elvis), Joshua Gibran Mayweather (Zero), Mena Suvari (Zoe), Gibby Haynes (Jujyfruit), Beverly D'Angelo (Dark's Mom), John Ritter (Moses Helper), Traci Lords (Val-Chick #1), Shannen Doherty (Val-Chick #2), Rose McGowan (Val-Chick #3), Keith Brewer (Surf), Derek Brewer (Ski), Roscoe (The Alien). Currently unavailable on DVD.

1999
Splendor

Cinematography: Jim Fealy. Director: Gregg Araki. Film Editing: Gregg Araki, Tatiana Riegel. Producers: Gregg Araki, Graham Broadbent, Damian Jones. Screenwriters: Gregg Araki, Jill Cargerman (additional voiceover). U.S. Release Dates: September 17, 1999 (New York City), October 1, 1999 (Los Angeles). With Kathleen Robertson (Veronica), Johnathon Schaech (Abel), Matt Keeslar (Zed), Kelly Macdonald (Mike), Eric Mabius (Ernest). Currently unavailable on DVD (previously released by Columbia TriStar).

2004
Mysterious Skin

Cinematography: Steve Gainer. Director: Gregg Araki. Film Editing: Gregg Araki. Producers: Gregg Araki, Jeffrey Levy-Hinte, Mary Jane Skalski. Screenwriter: Gregg Araki, based on the novel by Scott Heim. U.S. Release Date: May 6, 2005 (limited). With Joseph Gordon-Levitt (Neil McCormick), Brady Corbet (Brian Lackey), Bill Sage (Coach), Michelle Trachtenberg (Wendy), Jeff Licon (Eric), Mary Lynn Rajskub (Avalyn Friesen), Elisabeth Shue (Mrs. McCormick), Lisa Long (Mrs. Lackey), Chris Mulkey (Mr. Lackey), Ryan Stenzel (Stephen Zepherelli). Currently available on DVD from Strand Releasing.

2007
Smiley Face

Cinematography: Shawn Kim. Director: Gregg Araki. Film Editing: Gregg Araki, Alex Blatt. Producers: Gregg Araki, Steve Golin, Alix Madigan-Yorkin, Kevin Turen, Henry Winterstern. Screenwriter: Dylan Haggerty. U.S. Release Date: November 16, 2007 (limited). With Anna Faris (Jane F.), John Krasinski (Brevin), Danny Masterson (Steve the Roommate), Adam Brody (Steve the Dealer), Marion Ross (Shirley), John Cho (Mikey), Danny Trejo (Albert), Jane Lynch (Casting Director), Dylan Haggerty (Ferris Wheel Attendant), Scott 'Carrot Top' Thompson (Himself), Roscoe Lee Browne (Himself). Currently available on DVD from First Look Studios.

Bibliography

Aaron, Michele. "New Queer Cinema: An Introduction." *New Queer Cinema: A Critical Reader*. Ed. Michele Aaron. New Brunswick, NJ: Rutgers UP, 2004. 3-14.

"About the Production: *Nowhere*." Fine Line Features. 9 May 1997. 23 Aug. 1997 <http://www.flf.com/nowhere/notes/main.htm>.

Antani, Jay. Rev. of *Smiley Face*, dir. Gregg Araki. Filmcritic.com. 2007. 19 Mar. 2009 <http://www.filmcritic.com/misc/emporium.nsf/reviews/Smiley-Face>.

Araki, Gregg. "Filmmaker's Statement." *Totally F***ed Up DVD Insert*. New York: Strand Releasing, 2005. 7.

————. "Filmmaker's Statement." *The Living End: An Irresponsible Movie by Gregg Araki DVD Insert*. New York: Strand Releasing, 2008. 4.

————. "Production Notes." *Totally F***ed Up DVD Insert*. New York: Strand Releasing, 2005. 8-9.

————. "Production Notes." *The Living End: An Irresponsible Movie by Gregg Araki DVD Insert*. New York: Strand Releasing, 2008. 7.

————. "Spring 2005." *Totally F***ed Up DVD Insert*. New York: Strand Releasing, 2005. 12.

————. "Spring 2008." *The Living End: An Irresponsible Movie by Gregg Araki DVD Insert*. New York: Strand Releasing, 2008. 2.

————. "Synopsis." *The Living End: An Irresponsible Movie by Gregg Araki DVD Insert*. New York: Strand Releasing, 2008. 5.

————. "Totally F***ed Up." *Totally F***ed Up DVD Insert*. New York: Strand Releasing, 2005. 6.

————. "*Totally F***ed Up*: A Screenplay by Gregg Araki." New York: William Morrow, 1994.

Arnold, Matthew. "Culture and Anarchy." *Cultural Theory and Popular Culture: A Reader*. 2nd ed. Ed. John Storey. Athens: U of Georgia P, 1998. 7-12.

Arroyo, José. "Death, Desire, and Identity: The Political Unconscious of 'New Queer Cinema.'" *Activating Theory: Lesbian, Gay, Bisexual Politics*. Ed. Joseph Bristow and Angelia R. Wilson. London: Lawrence and Wishart, 1993. 70-96.

Asch, Andrew. "Teen Issues Meet Aliens in Director Gregg Araki's Mind." Knight-Ridder/Tribune News Service. 10 July 1997. 8 June 2000 <http://web2.infotrac.galegroup.com/itw/informark/715/229/65614186w3>.

Barthes, Roland, *Image, Music, Text*. New York: Hill and Wang, 1977.

Beaver, Frank. *Dictionary of Film Terms: The Aesthetic Companion to Film Analysis*. New York: Twayne, 1994.

Belton, John. *American Cinema/American Culture*. New York: McGraw-Hill, 1994.

Benshoff, Harry, and Sean Griffin. "Queer Cinema, the *Film* Reader: General Introduction." *Queer Cinema: The* Film *Reader*. Ed. Harry Benshoff and Sean Griffin. New York: Routledge, 2004. 1-15.

"Biography for Gregg Araki." Internet Movie Database. 2 Oct. 2008 <http://www.imdb.com/name/nm0000777/bio>.

Brodie, John. "Surprises Goose Sundance." *Variety* 13 Jan. 1997: 11.

Bryant, Wayne M. *Bisexual Characters in Film: From Anaïs to Zee*. Binghamton, NY: Harrington Park P, 1997.

Bywater, Tim, and Thomas Sobchack. *Introduction to Film Criticism: Major Critical Approaches to Narrative Film*. New York: Longman, 1989.

Chang, Chris. "Absorbing Alternative." *Film Comment* Sept.-Oct. 1994: 47-53.

Chonin, Neva. "Gregg Araki's Films Focus on Taboos, but His New One's Getting Mainstream Praise." *San Francisco Chronicle* 26 May 2005: E1.

Christopher, James. "Haunted by the Past." *The Times* 21 Oct. 2004: F14.

Cinema de Merde. Rev. of *Smiley Face*, dir. Gregg Araki. 11 Jan. 2007. 19 March 2009 <http://www/cinemademerde.com/Smiley_Face.shtml>.

Clare. Rev. of *The Doom Generation*, dir. Gregg Araki. 23 Dec. 2008 <http://www.mutantreviewers.com/rdoom.html>.

Clark, Kevin A. "Pink Water: The Archetype of Blood and the Pool of Infinite Contagion." *Power in the Blood: A Handbook on AIDS, Politics, and Communication*. Ed. William N. Elwood. Mahwah, NJ: Lawrence Erlbaum, 1999. 9-24.

Cooper, Dennis. "Baby Talky." *Artforum* May 1997: 22.

Custen, George F. "Strange Brew: Hollywood and the Fabrication of Homosexuality in *Tea and Sympathy*." *Queer Representations: Reading Lives, Reading Cultures*. Ed. Martin Duberman. New York: New York UP, 1997. 116-38.

Daly, Steve. Rev. of *The Doom Generation*, dir. Gregg Araki. *Entertainment Weekly* 10 Nov. 1995: 40.

D'Arcy, David. "Gregg Araki's Stoner Comedy." Greencine.com. 30 Dec. 2007. 19 Mar. 2009 <http://www.greencine.com/central.greggaraki>.

"Designed for Living." *Filmmaker Magazine*. Summer 1999. 30 June 2008 <http://www.filmmakermagazine.com/summer1999/splendor.php>.

Dossi, Joel. Rev. of *Mysterious Skin*, dir. Gregg Araki. *Cineaste* Summer 2005: 65-66.

Duralde, Alonso. "*The Living End* Lives Again: Gregg Araki's Sexy and Angry AIDS Road Movie Hits DVD in a Revamped New Edition." *Advocate* 6 May 2008: 65.

Ebert, Roger. Rev. of *The Doom Generation*, dir. Gregg Araki. Nov. 1995. 31 Jan. 2003 <http://www.suntimes.com/ebert/ebert_reviews/1995/11/1006063.html>.

Ehrenstein, David. "Gay Film's Bad Boy." *Advocate* 8 Sept. 2008: 70.

Elbaz, Mikhaël, and Ruth Murbach. "Fear of the Other, Condemned and Damned: AIDS, Epidemics, and Exclusions." *A Leap in the Dark: AIDS, Art, and Contemporary Cultures.* Ed. Allan Klusacek and Ken Morrison. Montreal: Véhicule P, 1993. 1-9.

Esther, John. "Gregg Araki: Tackling the Tough Ones on Film." *Gay and Lesbian Review* Sept.-Oct. 2005: 44-45.

Evans, Caroline, and Lorraine Gamman. "The Gaze Revisited, or Reviewing Queer Viewing." *A Queer Romance: Lesbians, Gay Men, and Popular Culture.* Ed. Paul Burston and Colin Richardson. New York: Routledge, 1995. 13-56.

Farber, Stephen. "A Drama of Family Loyalty, Acceptance—and AIDS." *New York Times* 18 Aug. 1985: 23+.

Farmer, Brett. *Spectacular Passions: Cinema, Fantasy, Gay Male Spectatorships.* Durham, NC: Duke UP, 2000.

Film.com. Rev. of *Nowhere,* dir. Gregg Araki. 1996. 23 Aug. 1997 <http://www.film.com/filma/reviews/ad_revw.idc?rev=1732>.

Film Fiend. Rev. of *The Doom Generation,* dir. Gregg Araki. 13 Aug. 2007. 23 Dec. 2008 <http://www/thefilmfiend.com/2007/08/doom-generation.html>.

Gleiberman, Owen. Rev. of *Splendor,* dir. Gregg Araki. *Entertainment Weekly* 8 Oct. 1999: 47.

Gonzalez, Ed. Rev. of *Mysterious Skin,* dir. Gregg Araki. *Slant* 3 May 2005. 26 Feb. 2009 <http://www.slantmagazine.com/film/film_review.asp?ID=1579>.

Green, Leila, and Sarah Goode. "The 'Hollywood' Treatment of Paedophilia." *Australian Journal of Communication* 35.2 (2008): 71-85.

Greene, Jane M. "Rethinking Screwball Comedy." *Film and Sexual Politics.* Ed. Kylo-Patrick R. Hart. Newcastle: Cambridge Scholars P, 2006. 7-27.

"Gregg's Going Somewhere." 30 May 1997. 23 Dec. 2008 <http://www.roughcut.com/main/drive1_97may5.html>.

Grundmann, Roy. "The Fantasies We Live By: Bad Boys in *Swoon* and *The Living End.*" *Cineaste* 19.4 (1993): 25-29.

Gunning, Tom. "An Aesthetic of Astonishment: Early Film and the (In)Credulous Spectator." *Film Theory and Criticism.* 6th ed. Ed. Leo Braudy and Marshall Cohen. New York: Oxford UP, 2004. 862-76.

Hall, Stuart. "Encoding/Decoding." *Culture, Media, Language: Working Papers in Cultural Studies, 1972-79.* Ed. Stuart Hall and Dorothy Hobson. London: Unwin Hyman, 1980. 128-38.

Halley, Stefan. "AFI Fest: Gregg Araki Puts on a Smiley Face." PopSyndicate.com. 2008. 19 Mar. 2009 <http://www.popsyndicate.com/archive/story/afi_fest_gregg_araki_puts_on_a_smiley_face>.

Hart, Kylo-Patrick R. *The AIDS Movie: Representing a Pandemic in Film and Television.* Binghamton, NY: Haworth P, 2000.

———. "Gay Male Spectatorship, Textual Flexibility, and Mainstream American Cinema." *Iowa Journal of Communication* 34.1 (2002): 1-26.

———. "Auteur/Bricoleur/Provocateur: Gregg Araki and Post-punk Style in *The Doom Generation.*" *Journal of Film and Video* 55.1 (2003): 30-38.

————. "Cinematic Trash or Cultural Treasure? Conflicting Viewer Reactions to the Extremely Violent World of Bisexual Men in Gregg Araki's 'Heterosexual Movie' *The Doom Generation*." *Journal of Bisexuality* 7.1-2 (2007): 53-69.

Hays, Matthew. "Make Art, Not Politics." *Montreal Mirror*. 17 July 1997. 13 Feb. 2009 <http://www.montrealmirror.com/archives/1997/071797/film1.html>.

————. *The View from Here: Conversations with Gay and Lesbian Filmmakers*. Vancouver: Arsenal Pulp P, 2007.

Hebdige, Dick. *Subculture: The Meaning of Style*. London: Routledge, 1991.

Heim, Scott. *Mysterious Skin*. New York: Harper, 1995.

Hershenson, Karen. "Bombs Away! Film Critic Hurls Invective across the Internet." Knight-Ridder/Tribune News Service. 1 Aug. 1997. 8 June 2000 <http://web2 .infotrac.galegroup.com/itw/infomark/715/229/65614186w3>.

Hundley, Jessica. "Apocalyptic Pop." Phoenix Media/Communications Group. June 1997. 13 Feb. 2009 <http://www.geocities.com/SoHo/Cafe/5214/araki.htm?200 913>.

Ide, Wendy. "Gregg Araki Pulls No Punches with *Mysterious Skin*." *The Times* 21 May 2005: F9.

indieWIRE. "Interview: 'Smiley Face' Director Gregg Araki." 16 Nov. 2007. 2 Oct. 2008 <http://www.indiewire.com/people/2007/11/indiewire_inter_125.html>.

"An Interview with James Duval." *The iMagazine*. 23 Jan. 1998 <http://www.eden .com/~soma/interview.html>.

Jacobs, Lea. *Wages of Sin: Censorship and the Fallen Woman Film, 1928-1942*. Berkeley: U of California P, 1997.

Jameson, Fredric. "Postmodernism and Consumer Society." *The Anti-Aesthetic: Essays on Postmodern Culture*. Ed. Hal Foster. Seattle: Bay P, 1983. 111-25.

Johnson, Heather. "Road Movies." GreenCine. 2006. 19 Mar. 2009 <http://www .greencine.com/static/primers/road.jsp>.

Justin. Rev. of *The Doom Generation*, dir. Gregg Araki. 23 Dec. 2008 <http://www .mutantreviewers.com/rdoom.html>.

Kaufman, Joanne. Rev. of *The Living End*, dir. Gregg Araki. *People* 9 Nov. 1992: 19.

Kenny, Glenn. Rev. of *The Doom Generation*, dir. Gregg Araki. *Entertainment Weekly* 31 May 1996: 68.

Klinger, Barbara. "The Road to Dystopia: Landscaping the Nation in *Easy Rider*." *The Road Movie Book*. Ed. Steven Cohan and Ina R. Hark. New York: Routledge, 1997. 179-203.

Koresky, Michael. Rev. of *Mysterious Skin*, dir. Gregg Araki. *Film Comment* May-June 2005: 73-74.

Kotek, Elliot V. "*Smiley Face* . . . and Gregg Araki." *Moving Pictures*. 2007. 19 Mar. 2009 <http://www.movingpicturesmagazine.com/festivities/articles/gregg araki>.

Kyle. Rev. of *The Doom Generation*, dir. Gregg Araki. 23 Dec. 2008 <http://www .mutantreviewers.com/rdoom.html>.

LaSalle, Mick. "Pedophile's Acts Beget Long Arc of Suffering." *San Francisco Chronicle* 27 May 2005: E5.

Lee, Michael J. "Gregg Araki and Scott Heim." *Radio Free Entertainment*. 24 May 2005. 26 Feb. 2009 <http://movies.radiofree.com/interviews/mysterio_gregg_araki_scott_heim.shtml>.

Leong, Ian, Mike Sell, and Kelly Thomas. "Mad Love, Mobile Homes, and Dysfunctional Dicks: On the Road with Bonnie and Clyde." *The Road Movie Book*. Ed. Steven Cohan and Ina R. Hark. New York: Routledge, 1997. 70-89.

Levy, Emanuel. "Nowhere." Rev. of *Nowhere*, dir. Gregg Araki. *Variety* 10 Feb. 1997: 66.

———. "Splendor." Rev. of *Splendor*, dir. Gregg Araki. *Variety* 15 Feb. 1999: 62.

———. *Cinema of Outsiders: The Rise of American Independent Film*. New York: New York UP, 1999.

Lim, Dennis. "AFI Fest: Zonked Out of Her Mind." *Los Angeles Times* 9 Nov. 2007. 19 Mar. 2009 <http://articles.latimes.com/2007/nov/09/entertainment/et-smiley 9>.

Lopez, Daniel. *Films by Genre*. London: McFarland, 1993.

McKinley, Will. "Put on a 'Smiley Face.'" *The Villager* 2-8 Jan. 2008. 19 Mar. 2009 <http://www.thevillager.com/villager_244/putasmiley.html>.

McQuail, Denis. *McQuail's Mass Communication Theory*. 4th ed. London: Sage, 2000.

Moran, James M. "Gregg Araki: Guerrilla Film-maker for a Queer Generation." *Film Quarterly* 50.1 (1996): 18-26.

Null, Christopher. Rev. of *The Doom Generation*, dir. Gregg Araki. 1999. 23 Dec. 2008 <http://www.filmcritic.com/misc/emporium.nsf/reviews/The-Doom-Generation>.

"Outspoken: Gregg Araki." *OutUK*. 26 Feb. 2009 <http://www.outuk.com/content/features/araki/index.html>.

Padgug, Robert A., and Gerald M. Oppenheimer. "Riding the Tiger: AIDS and the Gay Community." *AIDS: The Making of a Chronic Disease*. Ed. Elizabeth Fee and Daniel M. Fox. Berkeley: U of California P, 1992. 245-78.

Parish, James R., and Michael R. Pitts. *The Great Science Fiction Pictures*. Metuchen, NJ: Scarecrow P, 1977.

Pearl, Monica B. "AIDS and New Queer Cinema." *New Queer Cinema: A Critical Reader*. Ed. Michele Aaron. New Brunswick, NJ: Rutgers UP, 2004. 23-35.

"Personnel Bios." *Totally F***ed Up DVD Insert*. New York: Strand Releasing, 2005. 10-11.

Pomeranz, Margaret. "At the Movies: *Mysterious Skin*." 2005. 26 Feb. 2009 <http://www.abc.net.au/atthemovies/txt/s1198828.htm>.

PoolMan. Rev. of *The Doom Generation*, dir. Gregg Araki. 23 Dec. 2008 <http://www.mutantreviewers.com/rdoom.html>.

Porter, Edward. "Sensitive Skin." *Sunday Times* 22 May 2005: F15.

"Rebellious Love in the Age of AIDS." Rev. of *The Living End*, dir. Gregg Araki. Aug. 2008. 4 Dec. 2008 <http://gayinterestfilms.blogspot.com/2008/08/living-end-1992-usa-gregg-araki.html>.

Rich, B. Ruby. "The New Queer Cinema." *Sight and Sound* 2.5 (1992). Rpt. in *Queer Cinema: The Film Reader*. Ed. Harry Benshoff and Sean Griffin. New York: Routledge, 2004. 53-59.

————. "Vision Quest: Searching for Diamonds in the Rough." *Village Voice* 26 Mar. 2002: 43.

Russo, Vito. *The Celluloid Closet: Homosexuality in the Movies.* Revised ed. New York: Harper and Row, 1987.

Sarris, Andrew. "Notes on the Auteur Theory in 1962." *Film Theory and Criticism.* 6th ed. Ed. Leo Braudy and Marshall Cohen. New York: Oxford UP, 2004. 561-64.

Satuloff, Bob. Rev. of *Nowhere*, dir. Gregg Araki. *Advocate* 27 May 1997: 92.

Savlov, Marc. Rev. of *Splendor*, dir. Gregg Araki. *Austin Chronicle* 22 Nov. 1999. 13 Feb. 2009 <http://www.filmvault.com/filmvault/austin/s/splendor1.html>.

Schulman, Sarah. "Fame, Shame, and Kaposi's Sarcoma: New Themes in Lesbian and Gay Film." *My American History: Lesbian and Gay Life During the Reagan/Bush Years.* New York: Routledge, 1994. 228-32.

Schwarzbaum, Lisa. Rev. of *Nowhere*, dir. Gregg Araki. *Entertainment Weekly* 23 May 1997: 46.

Seguin, Denis. "Taboo or Not Taboo . . ." *The Times* 16 Oct. 2004: F17.

Severson, Matthew L. "Young, Beautiful, and F***ed." *Bright Lights Film Journal* 46 (1995). 23 Dec. 2008 <http://www.brightlightsfilm.com/15/araki.html>.

Shapiro, Benjamin. "Universal Truths: Cultural Myths and Generic Adaptation in 1950s Science Fiction Films." *Journal of Popular Film and Television* 18.3 (1990): 103-11.

Shumway, David R. "Screwball Comedies: Constructing Romance, Mystifying Marriage." *Film Genre Reader II.* Ed. Barry K. Grant. Austin: U of Texas P, 1995. 381-401.

Smith, Damon. "Rebel, Rebel." *Bright Lights Film Journal* 59 (2008). 4 Dec. 2008 <http://www.brightlightsfilm.com/59/59arakiiv.html>.

Smith, Gavin. "Sundance 'Kids.'" *Film Comment* Mar.-Apr. 1995: 8-9.

————. "Sundance 97: Digging for Gold." *Film Comment* Mar.-Apr. 1997: 55+.

Snyder, S. James. "This is Your Movie on Drugs." *New York Sun* 26 Dec. 2007. 19 Mar. 2009 <http://www.nysun.com/arts/this-is-your-movie-on-drugs/68563/>.

Straayer, Chris. *Deviant Eyes, Deviant Bodies: Sexual Re-orientation in Film and Video.* New York: Columbia UP, 1996.

Stringer, Julian. "Exposing Intimacy in Russ Meyer's *Motorpsycho!* and *Faster, Pussycat! Kill! Kill!*" *The Road Movie Book.* Ed. Steven Cohan and Ina R. Hark. New York: Routledge, 1997. 165-78.

Stuart, Jan. "Araki and a Hard Place." *Advocate* 12 Oct. 1999: 63.

Teeman, Tim. "Boys' Own Stories." *The Times* 19 May 2005: F19.

Thomson, Desson. "'Skin': Fearlessly Revealing." *Washington Post* 24 June 2005: WE34.

Wallenberg, Louise. "New Black Queer Cinema." *New Queer Cinema: A Critical Reader.* Ed. Michele Aaron. New Brunswick, NJ: Rutgers UP, 2004. 128-43.

Watney, Simon. *Policing Desire: Pornography, AIDS, and the Media.* 3rd ed. Minneapolis: U of Minnesota P, 1996.

Whitty, Stephen. "Totally F***ed Up." Knight-Ridder/Tribune News Service. 18 Aug. 1994. 8 June 2000 <http://web2.infotrac.galegroup.com/itw/infomark/715/229/65614186w3>.

Wollen, Peter. "The Auteur Theory." *Film Theory and Criticism*. 6th ed. Ed. Leo
    Braudy and Marshall Cohen. New York: Oxford UP, 2004. 565-80.
Wood, Robin. *Sexual Politics and Narrative Film: Hollywood and Beyond*. New
    York: Columbia UP, 1998.
Zion, Lawrie. "Child-abuse Film Faces Ban after Rating Dispute." *The Australian* 19
    July 2005: L4.
———. "Truth Lies Under the Skin." *The Australian* 3 Aug. 2005: F14.

Index

About the Author

Kylo-Patrick R. Hart (Ph.D., University of Michigan) is chair of the Department of Communication and Media Studies at Plymouth State University, where he teaches courses in film and television studies, video production, and popular culture. He is the author or editor of several books about media, including *The AIDS Movie: Representing a Pandemic in Film and Television, Film and Sexual Politics, Film and Television Stardom*, and *Mediated Deviance and Social Otherness: Interrogating Influential Representations*, as well as co-editor of *Media and the Apocalypse*.

Professor Hart was honored by being named the first-ever recipient of the Plymouth State University Award for Distinguished Scholarship. He values the opportunity to complete original research projects and remains quite active in this regard. His numerous research essays pertaining to film and television topics have appeared in various academic journals (including *Journal of Film and Video, The Journal of Men's Studies, Popular Culture Review*, and *Quarterly Review of Film and Video*) and media anthologies (including *Bang Bang, Shoot Shoot: Essays on Guns and Popular Culture; Common Sense: Intelligence as Presented on Popular Television; Gender, Race, and Class in Media: A Text-Reader; Men and Masculinities: Critical Concepts in Sociology;* and *Television: Critical Concepts in Media and Cultural Studies*). He is an enthusiastic member of the American Culture Association, the American Men's Studies Association, the National Communication Association, the Popular Culture Association, the Society for Cinema and Media Studies, the University Film and Video Association, and several additional academic and professional organizations.